TWAYNE'S WORLD AUTHORS SERIES
A Survey of the World's Literature

FRANCE

Maxwell A. Smith, Guerry Professor of French, Emeritus
The University of Chattanooga
Former Visiting Professor in Modern Languages
The Florida State University

EDITOR

Madame de Sévigné

TWAS 596

Madame de Sévigné

portrait by Claude Le Febvre
courtesy of the Musée Carnavalet

MADAME DE SÉVIGNÉ

By CHARLES G. S. WILLIAMS

The Ohio State University

TWAYNE PUBLISHERS

A DIVISION OF G. K. HALL & CO., BOSTON

Published in 1981 by Twayne Publishers,
A Division of G. K. Hall & Co.
All Rights Reserved

Printed on permanent/durable acid-free paper and bound
in the United States of America

First Printing

Library of Congress Cataloging in Publication Data

Williams, Charles G. S.
Madame de Sévigné.

(Twayne's world authors series; 596)
Bibliography: pp. 159-62
Includes index.
1.   Sévigné, Marie de Rabutin—Chantal, marquise de,
1626-1696.   2.   Authors, French—17th century—Biography.
I.   Title.   II.   Series.
PQ1925.W5   846'.4 [B]   81-4104
ISBN 0-8057-6438-0   AACR2

For my parents,
Earl and Thelma Williams,
who took me to Brittany

Contents

About the Author

Charles G. S. Williams is associate professor of Romance Languages at the Ohio State University. He received the B.A. from Kenyon College, M.Phil. and Ph.D. from Yale University. Recipient of a Fulbright fellowship to Oxford, he studied with the late W. G. Moore in St. John's and received B.A. and M.A. degrees from the University of Oxford. Professor Williams is the editor and a contributor to *Literature and History in the Age of Ideas: Essays on the French Enlightenment Presented to George R. Havens* and contributor of several sections to the supplement volume of the Cabeen seventeenth-century bibliography. He is also a member of the Ohio State University Press Board and the *French 17* bibliography committee. Recently he has completed a monograph on the seventeenth-century critic Valincour and is continuing research on the *Unigenitus* polemics begun with the support of the American Council of Learned Societies.

Preface

Mme de Sévigné forces any study of her letters to begin with
striking paradoxes. She became a writer, by accident, in middle
age. She never considered herself an "author." She expressed no
theory of writing. And she composed no "works" in the then
consecrated literary genres. Thousands of pages of her now famous
letters, written and cherished in privacy, at her death lay in ob-
scurity in the archives of her daughter's Château of Grignan.
Others were scattered through France. Now fewer than a hundred
remain in manuscript for editors and other readers who seek the
letter-writer in her hand and on her pages, written at speed, without
margins, and with little punctuation.

Given these paradoxes, and material difficulties they create,
Mme de Sévigné's literary fortunes have been unusually at the
mercy of editors, chance, and the prejudices or sympathies of class
and temperament of later readers. No seventeenth-century French
author long proclaimed "classic" has been more difficult to edit
and to know, to appreciate with adequate knowledge and to judge
with detachment. Only now, with the recently completed edition by
Professor Duchêne,[1] do we seem to have the "real" Mme de
Sévigné, insofar as it ever seems possible to fulfill that dream of
biographers.

The troubled history of the publication and reception of Mme de
Sévigné's letters has had to deal from the first with radical losses
and has itself been beset by paradoxes and controversy. Successive
discoveries of manuscript copies and rediscovery of the first
"unofficially" printed letters have only partially compensated for
destruction of manuscripts of mother and daughter, the latter
especially, destroyed for reasons now unclear by Mme de Sévigné's
granddaughter Pauline de Simiane. But those texts have at least
minimized mischief done by the eighteenth-century editor Denis-
Marius Perrin (with Mme de Simiane in the background). Those
guardians of textual propriety corrected and regularized usage,

bowdlerized daring thought and indiscreet confidence, excised and edited personal features of style. In short, they left us an incomplete record of the life of wit, presence, and inventive language that first brought Mme de Sévigné distinction and remain keys to her achievement as a writer.

Modified to mid-eighteenth-century taste, and for that reason in part a considerable publishing success already in the 1730s, the letter-writer became more proper (even "for the use of seminaries" in 1837), more to the taste of historians seeking revealing but respectable private views of a great reign, and finally more vulnerable. The qualities of wit, charm, and freedom of language seemed increasingly to some sober minds flaws, which excused rather than engaged "serious" claims to attention. Ernest Renan's dismissal of what he considered Mme de Sévigné's overinflated reputation—"Not even a thinker!"—is well known. Less so is another summary judgment by a woman of society, herself a brilliant letter-writer, the kind of reader who more often has made Mme la Marquise the object of a special cult. "Tittle-tattle," Lady Mary Wortley Montagu wrote to the Countess of Bute, "fashionable phrases," "endless repetitions," "gilt over by airy phrases, and a flowing style" (7.20.1754); "Very pretty the letters are, but I assert, without the least vanity, that mine will be full as entertaining forty years hence" (To Countess of Mar, June 1726). Voltaire agreed (To the D'Argentals, 9.23.1763), limiting appreciation to her wit, a very French pleasure he thought scarcely exportable; but to his English friend Falkener he recommended the letters among the best books "in regard to" French history (3.27.1752).

Reduced by an imperfect record and partial readings to a "literature of gossip," Mme de Sévigné's letters became and remain a source of enjoyment of that pleasure of anecdotal reality. As such they are a rich repository of historical fragments, sometimes a goad to denunciation (as by Breton patriots who hotly disputed her right to a national monument at Vitré in 1926), sometimes a matter of reserved uneasiness for literary historians. Less hesitatingly than they, a long list of writers, from Lamartine and Sainte-Beuve to Proust and Gide, through their own insights as writers, have admitted Mme de Sévigné to full community with the greatest writers of her time and beyond it. "This great lady, this robust and fertile letter-writer, in our age would probably have

been one of the great novelists,'' Virginia Woolf begins a portrait
of the letter-writer whose letters her own much resemble.

Beyond paradox and controversy, the fact is now evident that
Mme de Sévigné gave to French letters a uniquely rich and moving
personal correspondence. The letters in which she communicates to
her daughter in so many ways the substance of her love convey a
drama and poetry that give them a place among the great love
letters and ensure their writer's place among great writers, those
who have asked the most from the act of writing and given themselves most fully to its demands. The passion those letters express is
not the only passion in the world of Mme de Sévigné's letters, nor
the source of all its finest pages. But it is, in her own words, the
"center of life," a coherence that gave meaning to all its parts, just
as it gives a principle of higher, hidden order to the rambling "fine
disorder" of her letters.

Not least among paradoxes is the absence in print at present of
any book in English on Mme de Sévigné. Among the great writers
of the age of Louis XIV she has remained in the English-speaking
world the most neglected. In the two decades since Gérard-Gailly's
edition gave new life to her letters, however, debate in France on all
aspects of her art has brought about a rich renewal of study,
knowledge, and appreciation. The first concern of this book is to
bring to readers unable to have followed that renewal a chronolog-
ical presentation of Mme de Sévigné's letters that incorporates new
views and questions which have emerged since the 1950s.

It is a pleasure to acknowledge special indebtedness to the work
of Professor Roger Duchêne. For reading or listening to my early
drafts, I am grateful to Professor Edward Harvey of Kenyon
College, Thelma Williams, and my colleagues Mitchell Imhoff,
Martha Pereszlenyi, Sister Joann Recker, and Kay Shoulars.

CHARLES G. S. WILLIAMS

Columbus, Ohio

Chronology

1626	Birth in Paris of Marie de Rabutin-Chantal (February 5).
1627	Death of father, Celse de Rabutin, Ile de Ré (July 22).
1633	Death of mother, Marie de Coulanges (August 30). Maternal grandfather, Philippe de Coulanges, becomes guardian. Birth of favorite cousin, Philippe-Emmanuel de Coulanges.
1634	Birth of Mme de Lafayette, related to Sévignés by her mother's second marriage (December 1650).
1636	Death of Philippe de Coulanges (December 5).
1637	Uncle Philippe II de Coulanges made guardian (January 8).
1641	Last interviews, in Paris, with paternal grandmother, Mother de Chantal (d. December 13).
1644	Marriage to Henri, Baron de Sévigné (August 4). First voyage to family Château of Les Rochers in Brittany (August-November).
1646	Birth in Paris of Françoise-Marguerite de Sévigné (October 10).
1648	Birth of Charles de Sévigné at Les Rochers (March 12). The civil war of the Fronde begins (ended 1653), embroiling Sévigné family and finances.
1651	Henri de Sévigné dies (February 6) after duel.
1655	Visits Grande Mademoiselle at Saint-Fargeau.
1657	Portrayed as Clarinte in Mlle de Scudéry's *Clélie*.
1658	First reference to Mme de Sévigné's letters, by Costar.
1661	Arrest of Foucquet (September 5).
1663	Presentation at Court of Mlle de Sévigné, who dances in the Ballet of the Arts.
1664	Attends "Pleasures of the Enchanted Isle" at Versailles (May). Letters to Pomponne on Foucquet's trial. Voyage to her Château of Bourbilly in Burgundy (September-October).

1665 Bussy, her cousin, elected to French Academy. Clandestine publication of his *Amorous History of the Gauls*, containing a satirical portrait of Mme de Sévigné (as Mme de Cheneville). First edition of the *Maximes* of La Rochefoucauld, friend and family adviser.

1666 Bussy exiled to his estates in Burgundy.

1668 Charles departs for siege of Candia (September 26).

1669 Marriage of Mlle de Sévigné to the Comte de Grignan (January 29). Commission of standard-bearer in the Dauphin's guards purchased for Charles. Heavy borrowing imposes long-term financial strains. Grignan named Lieutenant-General of Provence. Miscarriage of Mme de Grignan (November).

1670 Birth of first grandchild, Marie-Blanche (November 15).

1671 *First Separation*: Departure of Mme de Grignan (February 4). Voyage to Les Rochers (May 18-December 9) of Mme de Sévigné. Birth of Louis-Provence de Grignan at Lambesc (November 17).

1672 First voyage of Mme de Sévigné to Grignan (July 30-October 5, 1673).

1674 Mme de Grignan in Paris (from February). Birth of Pauline de Grignan. Charles wounded in combat at Seneffe.

1675 *Second Separation*: Departure of Mme de Grignan (May 24). Mme de Sévigné at Les Rochers (September). Death of Turenne.

1676 First serious illness (rheumatism). First voyage to Vichy (May-June). Mme de Grignan gives premature birth (February 9) to second son (d. 1677). Cardinal de Retz, "head" of the family, retires to Commercy (June). Charles distinguished in army in Flanders (July). Return to Paris of Mme de Grignan, her health seriously altered (December). Beginning of the Affair of the Poisons.

1677 *Third Separation*: Departure of Mme de Grignan (June 8-December), with strained relations. Charles wounded at Valenciennes. Second voyage to Vichy (August-September). Leases the Carnavalet, with the Grignans.

1678 Publication of Mme de Lafayette's *La Princesse de Clèves*. Charles distinguishes himself at Mons (August).

1679 *Fourth Separation*: Departure of Mme de Grignan (September 13-November 1680). Death of Retz (August 24).

1680 Death of La Rochefoucauld (March 16), of Foucquet. Serious illness of Charles (August).

1683 Charles's sale of commission, retirement.

1684 Marriage of Charles to Marguerite de Mauron (February 8). *Fifth Separation*: Departure of Mme de Sévigné for Les Rochers (September 12).

1685 Return to Paris from Les Rochers (September 5). Rheumatism cured. Deaths of Duc du Lude, Comte de Guitaut.

1686? Presumed birth of the Grignans' last child, dead in infancy.

1687 Death of Christophe de Coulanges, uncle and financial adviser, the "Bien Bon" (August 29). *Sixth Separation*: Mme de Sévigné takes waters at Bourbon (September-October).

1688 *Seventh Separation:* Mme de Grignan departs (end September). Louis-Provence de Grignan in army at Philisbourg. Comte de Grignan given order of Saint-Esprit (December).

1689- Voyage to Chaulnes and last voyage to Les Rochers
1690 (April 14, 1689-September 24, 1690). Second voyage to Provence (arrival October 24).

1691 Return to Paris of Mme de Sévigné and the Grignans. "Year of infamies"—Grignans' financial collapse is imminent.

1693 Deaths of Bussy, Mme de Lafayette.

1694 *Eighth and Final Separation*: Departure of Mme de Grignan (March 25). Last voyage to Grignan (May).

1695 Marriages of Louis-Provence (January 2), of Pauline de Grignan to the Marquis de Simiane (December). Beginning of long illness of Mme de Grignan (July).

1696 Death of Mme de Sévigné (April 17) at Grignan, after a brief illness, most probably influenza.

The Letters

1696	First publication: Bussy's *Mémoires* (6 letters); with Bussy's *Lettres*, 1697 (109 letters).
1725	First independent edition: Troyes (28 letters).
1726	Two editions: 2v. Rouen (138 letters). Overseen by Amé-Nicolas, Bussy's elder son (Duchêne, I, 763); 2v. The Hague (177 letters).
1734–1737	"Official edition" by D.-M. Perrin. 6v. Paris: Simart (614 letters); Second edition, revised and augmented, 1754. 8v. Paris: Rollin (772 letters). On Perrin's editorial principles, Duchêne, I, 796-801.
1862	Edition Monmerqué-Régnier. 14v. Hachette, "Grands Ecrivains." First collective edition of the correspondence.
1876	Publication of Capmas MS., copies (ca. 1715-1719), overseen by Amé-Nicolas de Bussy-Rabutin, of 319 letters in their most complete and faithful texts (analysis by Duchêne, I, 789-92).

CHAPTER 1

Wealth (1626-1652)

I *A Beautiful Childhood*

MARIE de Rabutin-Chantal, future Marquise de Sévigné, was born on February 5, 1626, amid the solid comfort of the townhouse, now 1 bis Place des Vosges, which her maternal grandfather, Philippe de Coulanges, began to construct for his growing family in 1606. From its high windows, she had her first views of the world—the colorful townhouses like her grandfather's, presently the statue of Louis XIII, and the busy life of the most fashionable square in Paris. Summer was spent in equally fashionable Sucy-en-Brie. The family was large and closely knit, cheerfully enjoying together the revenues Coulanges received from capital shrewdly consolidated in administration of the state salt tax. Marriage of their eldest daughter, Marie, to Celse-Bénigne, Baron de Chantal—mother and father of the Marquise—was a tribute to the family's prosperity.

Baron de Chantal brought to the Coulanges family a double prestige: the aristocratic name Rabutin, noble since the twelfth century, and in the person of his mother the presence of a future saint. Jeanne de Chantal had left her family in 1610 to found, under the direction of Saint Francis of Sales, the Congregation of the Visitation-Sainte-Marie. But she watched with approval and pleasure the alliance of her son with the Coulanges. Blessed with these prayers and good health; supported by the love of a close family and material advantages they assumed with taste, wit, and spiritual values; ballasted by a good name, the happy paradise of the child held every promise for the future. Always faithful to the Coulanges, through this happy past, always spiritually at home in the Marais quarter, Mme de Sévigné came increasingly to need and to value her first guarantees of stability and happiness. From her

earliest years to widowhood at twenty-five, the inevitably perish-
able and fragile paradise of childhood was threatened by a series of
losses that seem to have recurred with almost fateful persistence.

Mlle de Chantal's first loss, at seventeen months, came with her
father's death. A dazzling swordsman, Chantal had distinguished
himself by his bravery and been rewarded by Louis XIII. Twice
compromised by illegal duels and by friendship with the Comte de
Chalais, executed in 1626 for conspiracy against Richelieu, Chantal
sought in defense of the island of Ré an opportunity to recoup his
waning fortunes at Court. He fought valiantly and fell in the field
of multiple wounds, from which he succumbed on July 22, 1627.

The Marquise de Sévigné had of her "brave and illustrious"
father (12.31.84) the image of a dashing soldier, preserved in his
portrait that remains at Les Rochers, and the inevitable fund of
family anecdotes. The Baron was "extremely high spirited," Bussy
recalled, "and had a style in everything he said that delighted those
around him, still more delighted by the ease and grace with which
he spoke." To the daughter from her father went an enjoyment of
a certain kind of sparkling, often mordant Rabutin wit, and with it
a name in which she took pride. To the young widow went a sizable
accumulation of debts, a contested inheritance, and the respon-
sibility of selling family lands.

At seven, Mlle de Chantal became an orphan. "I shall not pity
her," Mother de Chantal wrote to the Coulanges, "because I know
that you will be more than ever her true father and mother and that
your worthy sons will always cherish her."[1] Léonor de Rabutin,
intervening the first time in the fortunes of his niece, now an heiress
of consequence, agreed to Philippe's guardianship and to be
himself subrogate guardian. Life for the orphan scarcely changed,
and the image of her quietly devoted mother, never talked about in
the letters, seems to have been dimmed by the presence and devotion of others.[2] First Mme de Coulanges assumed the direction of
her granddaughter's first instruction and saw her first communion
at Saint Paul's in 1634, when Mother de Chantal wrote: "How
happy this little orphan will be if God will conserve you in your
wise and pious guidance of her; I love the child as I loved her
father, in God. I am especially joyful over the grace she will receive
from communion at Easter. I shall not fail to remember it and to
pray God that at this first reception of our sweet Saviour He will be

pleased to take entire possession of this little soul and make it forever his" (VII, 315). Already ill, Mme de Coulanges died in early May, less than two years before her husband followed her to the crypt beneath the family chapel in the church of the Visitation convent in the rue Saint-Antoine. The house on the Place des Vosges was sold; and with these losses the child's world did change.

A family council of sixteen, assurance against real insecurity, convened first on January 8, 1637. From fear of conflict of interest in settling the inheritance, Léonor de Rabutin opposed a Coulanges guardian for his niece and proposed exclusive guardianship by her father's family. The cheerful and worldly Coulanges household would be exchanged for the somber Château of Monthelon in Burgundy and a foster mother, Comtesse de Toulongeon, whose avarice was already a source of gossip. With that guardianship Mlle de Chantal might well have found herself in a Visitation convent, in spite of the fact that neither her temperament nor precocious gifts suggested any vocation for the religious life. If other interests prevailed, she might have found a different future. Her cousin Bussy, who had just distinguished himself in his first campaigns, needed a dowry that would further a military career worthy of his name, promise, and ambitions.

The bishops of the family were more inclined to gamble on the Coulanges' true qualities and the advantages of their continued guardianship: Philippe II was appointed guardian and his brother Christophe, Abbé de Livry, began fifty years of account keeping that the Marquise acknowledged at his death to have been the bedrock of all her "ease and serenity."[3] Philippe's young wife, Marie Lefèvre d'Ormesson, sister of the magistrate and journal writer Olivier, offered a continued education that fostered an adolescence quite different from that promised by Mme de Toulongeon. "Entire freedom to do as she wished" (VII, 620), it seemed to a momentarily worried Mother de Chantal, was what the orphan found in her changed but familiar surroundings.

As predicted, Philippe II gladly accepted his niece into his household in the rue des Francs-Bourgeois that included her young Coulanges uncles as regular guests. In the gardens at Sucy, she played sometimes with seven of her Coulanges, d'Ormesson, and La Trousse cousins, and from 1637 until her marriage seven years later, Mlle de Chantal continued to enjoy security, love, and freedom. Amid the joys of Sucy, where she seemed a young "beauty to win all hearts," Mme de Sévigné was given the most precious of all gifts, the natural development of her own personality. These first joys of the country's abundant nature were later remembered, and with them another scarcely separable from them in childhood memories, the joy of a love freely given to and by the child and adolescent. "How could you not love me?" she wrote to her favorite cousin, the impish versifier Philippe-Emmanuel de Coulanges, whom in memory of Sucy she addressed playfully as "my child" long after his middle-age. "Loving me," she recalled, "was the first thing you did when you opened your eyes, and it was I who began the fashion of loving you" (4.26.95). It is a part of the moving drama of her letters that Mme de Sévigné was unable to recapture and ensure for her children the untarnished paradise of her own childhood.

No woman in the Coulanges family was forced by necessity to embrace the conventual life. But from first communion until marriage, arranged by the Abbé de Coulanges and the future Cardinal de Retz ten years later, Mlle de Chantal heard Mass in the family chapel whose foundation consecrated in 1634 the family's bond with the Visitation convent. Her early presence in the convent (where three of Foucquet's sisters and his aunt resided), without the restraints of its order, may have done more than years of the structured program of a boarder there to prepare Mlle de Chantal for her later life.

The child and young woman might see in the convent, as in her grandparents' household, a religion that was both respected *and* loved. It was the kind of religion Pascal thought the only one able to draw certain worldly persons toward the fullness of religious experience, and enduring childhood memories disposed Mme de Sévigné to wish to make an appropriate place, beyond ritual observance, for the presence of that kind of religion in her life. She sought in convents of the Visitation moments of spiritual quietude. But alarmed that her granddaughter Pauline might be made a boarder, she wrote in dismay to Mme de Grignan: "Oh! my daughter, keep her with you! Don't believe that a convent can rectify an education—either on the subject of religion, which our sisters scarcely know, or on other things. You will do better at Grignan, when you have the time to put yourself to it. Have her read good books . . . since she is bright and talk to her" (1.24.89).

Imagining that Pauline's "pretty, natural wit" made her resemble her grandmother temperamentally, Mme de Sévigné wished for her the privileges of a childhood as free as her own had been. That freedom would lead her also to a sense of the fullness of life and provide inner resources necessary to renew that life after suffering its losses.

In 1641 losses continued for Mlle de Chantal. First came the death of Archbishop André Frémyot, her scholarly great-uncle. In retirement from the see of Bourges he had cherished his niece all the more after the death of her father, whom he had treated as a son. In his library, nearby in the Place des Vosges, the young girl was welcome and could find serious books of history, biography, and moral philosophy that came to mean much to her in later troubled times. Within six months of this death, Mother de Chantal died at Moulins. But it remained for the woman Mme de Sévigné to find, to her surprise, from other losses—of husband and daughter—that "life is cruelly mixed with bitterness." For the adolescent, as Mme de Sévigné later recalled, the joy of living of a "beautiful child- hood" (7.22.76) remained untinged.

II   *Fête Galante*

Serious learning was not, in France in the 1630s, women's business. After examining the education women received, at all levels of society, the historian Gustave Fagniez concluded that what is most conspicuously absent from it is training and cultivation of the mind, the very core of the best education available to men. Precedence was given to instruction on religious duty and its accomplishment and to domestic arts, knowledge that allowed women to withstand "temptations" and to flourish as overseers of the household.[4]

One striking example of flattering condescension that scarcely masks the prejudice of women's intellectual inferiority is offered by the foreword to *The Ladies' Library*, published by the hack writer Grenaille in 1640. "Your minds are too good," he begins coyly, "not to need to read, and your eyes are too beautiful to read con- stantly. I present you with a little library that may dispel boredom while offering some pleasant moments of instruction. Leave your novels a bit and find some excellent truths here, think less of your usual pleasure than of your salvation." The pious texts included, modernized and bowdlerized, edifying rather than instructive, are offered as correctives of frivolity; and the proper scope of women's reading is set. In short, for a woman of any standing, the goal of education is "to erect a beautiful temple to virtue, within her soul as in her person." Shorter still, we may see, proper education is simply to learn to be an honorable daughter, wife, and widow in men's eyes, and with his anthology Grenaille published tracts on all three.

Mlle de Chantal's education, the gift of freedom to grow naturally in mind and spirit, by contrast with Grenaille's fatuous moralizing seems like the constantly renewed invitation to a ball. The family council set aside 1,200 livres, later 1,800, for "payment of the masters who would instruct her." A whole procession of now nameless masters must have shared this handsome sum, with better grace and effect than the lot assembled by Molière for his bourgeois, would-be gentleman, M. Jourdain. Singing and dancing masters there must have been, since Mme de Sévigné sang with pleasure songs whose difficulty required prior basic instruction and executed dances that even her natural grace could not alone have mastered. A riding master did his job. She rode well, with energetic equestriennes like the Duchesse de Sully, but with limited enthusiasm: "Most ills," she quipped, "come from keeping one's backside in the saddle" (8.26.71). Language masters were certainly employed. Mlle de Chantal learned enough Latin to appreciate Virgil (with the aid of an Italian translation),[5] some Spanish, and fluent Italian. After reading Tasso on a long afternoon at Les Rochers, she spoke of her "good masters" (6.21.71, without identification). Two distinguished men, Jean Chapelain and Gilles Ménage, have traditionally been identified as those masters, the only ones to have left a signature on the accomplishments of their "pupil." But the contributions of both men are in fact uncertain and seem to have offered "further" rather than first education.

Chapelain, once preceptor in the household of Mme de Sévigné's aunt, the Marquise de La Trousse, remained a frequent visitor through the 1630s—but certainly would not have accepted a similar post in 1637, when he had gained stature as an academician and critic. Informal interest in Mlle de Chantal may have led the friend of the family to offer bits of casual assistance in language study, some suggestions for reading, and commentary on literary events.

It seems to have stopped there. He had occasion to offer her cousin, the Chevalier de La Trousse, another kind of advice: "Take care," he admonished, "to write your journal—and your letters—in the most artistic manner." It was not suitable advice for a woman and was not offered to Mlle de Chantal.[6]

When Ménage first met the fourteen-year-old Mlle de Chantal, he was a silver-haired, svelte man of twenty-seven, who with his aggressive snaps of wit and cultivated lapses of taste was no model for a comic pedant. Already established, before introduction into the Coulanges' drawingroom by Chapelain, as "tutor" he was probably as informal as his mentor and offered much the same kind of tuition. Like Chapelain he remained an old friend after Mlle de Chantal's marriage, indeed "the best of best friends," she promised with a special flourish of the pen. From games of blindman's-bluff, Ménage moved on to a ritual game of poetic courtship that he, unlike his partner, came to take seriously. In matters of style, epistolary or other, he really had nothing to teach the young woman. She already knew the steps he asked her to dance, and when the mime of courtship evolved to an exchange of letters, some solid practice with her cousin Bussy already lay behind the "further education" of the epistolary skirmish.

Of a tutor of philosophy, or in general a more formal and rigorous intellectual training, there is no trace. A revolution in philosophy and science went by Mlle de Chantal without its being thought by her guardian or her, then or later, to be really any of her business. Descartes occupied her only late and momentarily, for the special reason of communication with her daughter; and, when faced with the demands of reading Malebranche, she threw up her hands, "I'll not pretend, foolishly," she declared, "to be a learned woman when I am not" (6.15.80). Learned women remained for her, as for her time, more or less admirable curiosities. Once first education had given the granddaughter of Jeanne de Chantal fittingly solid religious instruction and knowledge of domestic affairs, which served well in overseeing her estates, she settled down to the staples of fashionable ladies' reading Grenaille describes and found greatest pleasure in D'Urfe's *L'Astrée* and other novels, urbane verse, and the grandeur of Corneille's plays.

However inestimably precious the freedom of Mlle de Chantal's education, and however seemingly free from conventionality, it imposed its own limitations upon her mind, her imagination, even her spirit, and shaped her life quite conventionally. Raised as she was, the power to find a new focus and equilibrium through the mind—that a Mme de La Sablière or later Mme du Châtelet found through science and philosophy—was no more there for Mme de Sévigné than was the capacity to lose herself in dreams or devotion. The gardens of *L'Astrée* and the meditations of the Jansenist Nicole offered delightfully different settings for refreshing strolls. But neither the banks of the Lignon nor the valley of Port-Royal replaced the gardens of Sucy or Livry, Paris, Les Rochers, and the Château of Grignan as the true abodes of her spirit.

Judging from the journal kept by Philippe-Emmanuel de Coulanges at his father's bidding, and at greater distance from Mme de Sévigné's letters on her granddaughter's education, education directed by Philippe de Coulanges was animated by the spirit of Montaigne. It was an education for self-reliance, as a means to happiness. Belief in the value of books and wide reading, and of the mind to find its pleasures freely, was the key to a healthy mind, a vital force in the integrated person who can live in the world, as Montaigne wished, fittingly and easily. If freedom did not extend to the grand tour that capped her cousin's education, Mlle de Chantal did travel with her uncle and was no more isolated from experience of the world beyond the Coulanges' drawingroom than she was sheltered in it from books and ideas. In 1640 she accompanied him to Normandy, where the facts of desolation and suffering left in the wake of insurrection over tax levies could not have been concealed from her.

The experience that shaped her adolescence was reaffirmed in later life. "Not to find pleasure in serious readings gives pastel colorings to the mind" (11.16.89), she felt; but she continued to love the pastels of her youth, in the verses of Benserade and Voiture, for example, that colored her speech. Reading remained what it first was, an agreement of life, to be worn with the other graces to ornament its performances. But age also deepened Mme de Sévigné's early conviction that in her reading, as in her speech and dress, bold basic colors were both suitable and becoming.

The religion Mlle de Chantal knew, one lovable as well as venerable, the love she had been given "without detachment," and a life open to joys in her world seem to have closed her heart to her grandmother, her life and the mysticism it symbolized. The first biographer of the saint describes her last visit to Paris in a manner that may assure us of the chill Mlle de Chantal felt upon leaving the Coulanges' drawingroom for her last interviews with her grandmother. Seeing her granddaughter infrequently and only "to satisfy the duties of charity she felt obliged to give to her spiritual needs, judge," Bishop Maupas du Tour asked his readers, "what virtue our holy widow had . . . to surmount in herself the most delicate and legitimate feelings of nature."[7]

Judge it Mlle de Chantal may have done, perhaps with the echo of Corneille's chilling portrayal of the surmounting of legitimate feelings of nature in his *Horace* a year earlier, perhaps with the memory that her grandmother was obliged to walk over the prostrate body of her protesting son in order to follow the call of an imperious vocation.[8] The woman, like the adolescent, remained mystified, perhaps repelled, before the scandal of this absolute spiritual claim, whose autonomy was never felt possible in her own life. She does not seem to have felt the spirit of Saint Francis's new order, the new option it gave to a woman, say a young widow, to find freedom *in* society through spiritual autonomy.[9] With her heart open to maternal love, indeed laid bare to it, the grandeur of the vocation of a heart aflame with another love remained closed to the widow Sévigné. It was not until two years before her death, and then only with the echo of her own daughter's words in her mind, that she wrote: "You move me when you speak of my grandmother's heart. It was filled with the love of God" (4.5.94). But feelings of the intermittence of the heart, of a heart divided by the struggle of two loves, break into Mme de Sévigné's life in some of the most moving letters that she wrote.

Another more worldly scene, recorded by d'Ormesson, gives the proper setting for the promise of happiness bright in the beauty of the fiancée, a sumptuous scene in which Mlle de Chantal seems the perfect vision of all that a Grenaille might wish: "In the evening at the Minims, the day of Saint Francis of Paola: My father dined there with many friends of the House; they were well treated. The Queen came to vespers. The Bishop of Uzès preached, the King's music was excellent, Mlle de Chantal gathered alms" (*Journal*, 4.5.44). But an even more splendid scene awaited, which crowned with ultimate (and conventional) success the education that had prepared her to take her place in society with distinction. The Renaissance Chapel to the Virgin in the Church of Saint Gervais, illuminated at two o'clock in the morning, reflected the radiance of the young couple, Marie de Rabutin-Chantal and Henri de Sévigné, joined in matrimony on August 4, 1644, by the Bishop of Chalon, the bride's great-uncle.

Of a nobility that had sent a knight on the Seventh Crusade, the groom was at twenty-one only three years older than his bride. Handsome, orphaned also, possessing from a diminished inheritance "yet a good balance of about 40,000 livres," he seems the embodiment of a romanesque hero. And, to boot, Bussy reported, "he wanted always to be in love." The bride, of course, expected just that and, after many balls, the final invitation to a *"fête galante."* She was ready to move with equal grace and distinction through the Hôtels of Rambouillet and Richelieu, the salon of the Grande Mademoiselle, the drawingrooms of Mme du Plessis or Pomponne, the society of Retz and La Rochefoucauld—on the margin of society through formal provincial functions in Brittany or at its heart in the Court itself.

III   *Abyss*

After a three-month honeymoon in Brittany, which gave the new Baroness de Sévigné (Marquis was her husband's courtesy title) her first tour of family lands, the young couple leased the first floor of a house, now 14 rue des Lions, that remained their home in Paris for their entire married life. It was the first in the series of rented residences culminating with the Carnavalet (1677) in which Mme de Sévigné, the mistress of numerous estates and of Bourbilly in her own right, chose to pass her life in the Marais quarter. At 525 francs a year, it was well beneath the manner to which the bride might have felt herself accustomed and was not spacious enough to entertain on the scale the Sévignés were entertained elsewhere.

Lavishly entertained they of course were. The luxuriant pleasures of Paris, of the "bonny Regency," as it always remained in Mme de Sévigné's fond memories, are legendary. And it was the aristocratic and magisterial circles in which the new couple moved, most threatened with crises of values and existence by the asperity of Richelieu's last years, that basked most freely and extravagantly in the pleasures of the new society. Although in 1643 Henri de Sévigné had borrowed 4,000 francs for horses and other requirements of a military campaign (not repaid until 1652 by his widow),[10] ambition to take advantage of them was lacking. Freed from the past, a solitary and bleak Breton childhood, he became passionately addicted to his new life. His wife, for whom the pleasures of the new society were natural, by all indications, found her passion in him. "There are good marriages but no delicious ones," La Rochefoucauld remarked acidly, but the Sévignés at least promised to be an exception.

"The heart would like Paris," Mme de Sévigné confessed, "but the head says Brittany" (8.21.89), a practical truth learned in early years of marriage but never accepted without a sense of sacrifice. Already in 1646 Bussy teased the young couple that at Les Rochers they had found either a bower of bliss or philosophical retreat, knowing full well the real reason for their year's absence from Paris: ". . . Your household/Set up in the village/Makes your capital stretch where it never stretched before." "When one doesn't stay on one's land and be nourished by it, I don't very well know how one can manage," Mme de Sévigné often had to admit (for example, 12.27.84). For this reason among others half of her married life was spent in Brittany.

Given the terms of her marriage contract, and the fact that Mme de Sévigné's estate was in 1696 appraised at 593,000 livres,[11] it seems against all justice for the new household to be troubled from the first by financial difficulties, increasingly serious and finally critical. At first the Sévignés must have felt little need and less inclination for rigorous calculation of a budget. But to make their extravagance, much less Sévigné's philandering, solely responsible for their financial disarray is a fiction that seems too convenient.

During the Sévignés' marriage constantly spiraling inflation combined with nonpayment of interest on municipal bonds placed constraints of limited capital on all persons living, as they were, predominantly on interest from investments. With the tightening of fiscal machinery to finance the Franco-Spanish war followed by the interferences of the civil war of the Fronde, interest payments, already poorly and irregularly paid by 1644, all but ceased and were never during Henri de Sévigné's lifetime restored with regularity.[12] Bad harvests and added tax burdens reduced the monetary profit from dependents on estates, whose direct payments were in the best times difficult to collect, and that profit was further diminished by self-seeking agents who mismanaged their estate of Buron near Nantes in the absence of its owners. "I cry famine atop a mound of

grain" (10.21.73), Mme de Sévigné wrote later from Burgundy, in
times no more difficult than the first years of her marriage had
been. And from Brittany she complained, with characteristic
resignation to the loss of money owed to her: "I see persons everywhere who owe me money and who have no bread, who sleep on
straw and weep. What would you have me do to them?" (6.9.80).
For the Sévignés, cash was short, income uncertain. Complicated
credit schemes were obligatory. If at Henri's death two years' rent,
servants' wages, even sizable linen bills were outstanding among
other debts, high living alone had obviously not caused them to be.

The civil war of the Fronde brought other difficulties to the
Sévignés: nobody of their class, we know now, was ever quite the
same after the Fronde. Once awakened by it, Henri's ambition was
badly directed. He chose to follow the Duc de Longueville, whose
ambitions Retz judged "infinitely beyond his capabilities" and
inflated by pressures from his wife. Longueville's march to Rouen,
in January 1646, to incite his dependents and to assure the alle-
giance of the *Parlement*, proved to be a fool's errand, and Henri
distinguished himself dubiously by playing the fool. "When he discovered that being *maréchal de camp* didn't require his skill,"
Saint-Evremond reported, "he set himself up as a jester and had
the honor of making His Highness laugh."[13]

Bussy teased his cousin about becoming politically engaged, but
she was decidedly no Mme de Longueville. Some of the bad days of
the Fronde were spent in Brittany; and when she did attend with
d'Ormesson stormy sessions of *Parlement*, the pleasure of ob-
serving a dramatic moment (along with fiscal self-interest) may well
have drawn her there. A taste for intrigue she seems never to have
had to any degree, though perfectly capable of it, and military
prowess for its own sake seldom gave her any particular feeling of
exaltation. Anticipating her feelings, Bussy wrote during the Paris
blockade in March: "The war is beginning to bore me thoroughly,
and unless you die quickly of famine I shall die of weariness"
(3.5.49). In mock alarm he professed fear that the continuation of
divided family allegiances (he was serving under Condé) would
force her to break family ties in the manner of Corneille's Horace
(2.7.49). But there was no real need for concern. Both the Sévignés
were doubtless relieved when the redirection of Henri's ambition
led to the purchase in June of the charge of governor of Fougères,
with his wife's signature as guarantor of the half-unpaid cost of

60,000 livres, a charge never really assumed and that remained to be dealt with after his death. The purchase of that office may indicate that the debit from being on the wrong side was not a serious one; there was yet, however, the presence of Retz to increase it appreciably.

Admiration for extraordinary qualities of energy and mind, respect, real affection, and concern are the feelings for Retz that pervade Mme de Sévigné's letters. From her marriage to the first moment of widowhood, when his Paris residence served as her address, Retz was there as head of the family, sustainer of its hopes and fortunes, to whom she was always and almost puzzlingly loyal. She may have heard on January 25, 1659, at Saint Paul's the inflammatory invective of his sermon attacking Mazarin, which to many seemed a scandal. She certainly followed his public reverses with sympathy, from the defeat in 1649 of his regiment, led by her uncle Renaud de Sévigné, to his final retirement to Commercy and a much contested "conversion" that she defended. She knew much less than we, as readers of his *Mémoires*, which she almost certainly never knew,[14] about the workings of Retz's mind and political stratagems. Whatever she knew, she and her family may also have known some of his discredit. Forgiven Retz may have been, but his opposition to Mazarin was never forgotten by the minister or by Louis XIV, who finally became the real hope and sole arbiter of the family's fortune.

Given the debits of the Fronde, attachment to Jansenism first formed in Mme de Sévigné's married years through her husband's family seems a negligible addition. Jansenist piety offered her a new kind of meditation and solace. But her enthusiasm for Jansenism as a cause (hidden with effort) was potentially dangerous and compromising in the face of inflexible royal opposition to it. She knew that for the good of her family such opinions dictated by loyalty (like defense of Bussy against royal displeasure) had better remain matters of conscience. At those tactical moments she made some effort to restrain a freedom to say what she wished, always cherished and enjoyed during married years to the point of scandal.

If it seems unjust that Mlle de Chantal should have been plagued with financial difficulties, it seems even more so that the "beauty to win all hearts" should have been distressed by infidelities that clouded the last years of marriage. Her head was not so clouded by romance that she expected the life of the man she had married, in the society in which they found their pleasures, to be free from all dalliance. But just as surely she did not expect to play the part that Sévigné's weakness, more than anything else, forced upon her, to the scandal of the supreme collector of scandals, Tallemant des Réaux.

Henri de Sévigné, Tallemant decided, "was not a gentleman," not nearly good enough for his wife; Bussy, for his part, concluded simply that Sévigné indeed had bad taste.[15] Perhaps there was no scandal for Mme de Sévigné that her husband trailed off after the most glamorous courtesan of the day, Ninon de Lenclos. She wrote to Mme de Grignan that Ninon had "spoiled" Henri (3.13.71), not ruined him. It would have taken a stronger man than Sévigné to resist the seductive aggressiveness of the woman reported to have said, "Since I see that men take the best things for themselves, I hereby make myself a man," and to have kept her advances a secret. And it would have taken a different woman from the twenty-three-year-old Mme de Sévigné to counter those advances. "M. de Sévigné respects me but doesn't love me; I love him but don't respect him," Tallemant reports her to have remarked calmly. Ninon, whose taste was for good conversation and adventure, also had a special penchant for chestnut-colored hair. She happened to see Henri de Sévigné, she wanted him, and she had him (for the usual three-month term allotted lovers who brought neither good conversation nor adventure). Expense, like scandal, was spared; Ninon accepted only a ring. Neither was spared by Belle Lolo, Mme de Gondran, to whom Sévigné next fell prey. A beautiful but mindless adventuress, who involved him with her husband in a *ménage-à-trois* that bemused and revolted society, it was a slendor honor Sévigné gave up his life to defend. The final duel with the Chevalier d'Albret was pointless and based on a ridiculous misunderstanding.[16]

One month before her seventh anniversary, on her twenty-fifth birthday, Mme de Sévigné became a widow. Françoise-Marguerite was only four; Charles, not yet three. Did her new loss make her feel more oppressively the long list of past losses? Loss of happiness was real, when she recalled "the abysses in which M. de Sévigné left me" (11.13.87), to the surprise of many who expected her to feel only relief. Loss of happiness was only one part of the complex debits exacted by the seven-year balance-sheet of marriage. Although the continuing upheavals of the Fronde offered no grounds for optimism, renewed assumption of the management of her affairs by the Abbé de Coulanges relieved some anxiety. One more menacing debit remained for the "honorable widow": in the society that had undone her husband, Mme de Sévigné herself had not been able to escape compromising gossip.

Loret's *Muse historique* (7.16.60) archly informed its readers that Mmes de Sévigné, Fiesque, and Montglas were about to be banished from the Prince d'Harcourt's drawingroom for being too "loose in speech" (*guillerette*). This publicity in company with Bussy's future mistress and the forever coy Comtesse de Fiesque, skewered by one of Mme Cornuel's malicious one-liners ("She keeps her beauty because her folly has preserved it in salt.") and preserved in Bussy's *Amorous History of the Gauls*, may at the moment have seemed less than serious. It was tantamount to an advertisement of coquetry, but that was scarcely news to the readers of the *Muse*. Coquetry for the woman who had been so lavishly admired as a child and adolescent was as natural as laughter. More than one society poet (Saint-Pavin, Montreuil, Ménage) had sung Mme de Sévigné's charms, and the merry dance she led Ménage was not entirely private. A procession of genial rogues, in whose company she enjoyed shining, also file through her letters. And the attentions of at least one notoriously fickle womanizer, Henri de Daillon, Comte du Lude, who remained her friend, set tongues wagging more than the publicity of the *Muse*, renewed on June 23, 1652, by the announcement that the Marquis de Tonquedec and Duc de Rohan had almost come to blows over "Cévigny la belle." Even at sixty she was courted, by Louis-Charles de Luynes, who proposed that she become the third Duchesse de Luynes (8.1.85). She "likes men in general," and "prefers being paid court to being offered friendship," Bussy observed; and with her widowhood, his letters keep us informed, suitors abounded who were pleased to comply with her preference.

There are coquettes and coquettes, as Bussy is at pains to distinguish in the new *Satyricon* of his *Amorous History*. Henri de Sévigné may have been cuckolded in the eyes of God, Bussy remarks, savoring poetic justice, but in the eyes of his contemporaries he managed to avoid appearing so in fact. A great distance separates the flirtatious woman who remains honorable from the rapacious predators that use "last favors" as capital investments and extortion, the distance between Molière's Célimène and

Bussy's Comtesse d'Olonne or Duchesse de Châtillon. Mme de
Sévigné remained among the honorable women, a Célimène without a humiliating "fifth act," and remained so without hiding
behind a mask of prudery the pleasures she always felt in the
company of handsome men. How could Mlle de Chantal have
become a prude? By self-defense and maternal protectiveness? If
the abysses to which Henri de Sévigné, and her own temperament,
took her included the moral jungle that undergrew the pleasures of
the "bonny Regency," Mme de Sévigné for the most part con-
trived henceforth to keep herself well away from its edge and gossip
endangering her children's future.

Immediately after her husband's death, Mme de Sévigné transported her grief, future problems, and children to Les Rochers and
took inventory there. The Sévigné lands and Les Rochers itself,
the regular family residence for two centuries, had not substantially
changed since her honeymoon.[17] The Château, on a promontory
surrounded by woodland and meadows, did not yet have the
present gracious air given by eighteenth-century renovations. The
two wings extending south and east from the central tower and
outer tower to the northwest (where Mme de Sévigné's apartment
may still be visited) were yet surrounded by the full panoply of
medieval fortifications. The gracefully harmonized south wing did
not yet stretch toward the hexagonal tower chapel capped in blue
slate, the pride and plan of the Abbé de Coulanges finished only in
1675. The busy life of the farm and woods, where occasionally a
wolf was sighted, must have seemed as it did to the new bride both
more domestically rustic and more wild than the lawns of Sucy and
the copses of Livry. Ten acres of courtyards, woods, and almost
sixty acres of farmland and meadows beyond to the north and the
east toward the parish church of Etrelles must also have given the
young Parisian the feeling of openness and freedom.

Over the years there were to be many changes at Les Rochers.
The walled garden to the west, laid out from Le Nôtre's design,
with its orange trees, trick echo corner, and sundial took the shape
of Mme de Sévigné's plan. In the first year of her widowhood, the
dark forest beyond the garden gate began to be cleared for the
planting of beech and chestnut trees that with time formed ten
interlocking walkways, "a solitude made expressly for proper
meditation" (9.29.75). The seeds of a new life were also planted
lovingly by Mme de Sévigné in the lives of her children.

The widow's return to Paris was again news. Recovered from her grief but still showing signs of it, "young, beautiful, chaste as a turtle-dove," the *Muse* celebrated her welcome return to the other beauties of the salons. The woman whose life followed conventionally the archetypal pattern of daughter, wife, mother and widow had other plans for the difficult task of safeguarding independence, for the sake of her children. After her husband's death, the "holy widow" Jeanne de Chantal, by a symbolic act that imposed her vocation and removed her from the society in which she might be expected to find a second husband, had burnt JESUS in inch-high letters across her breast. The widow Sévigné chose to remain in society, that she loved and needed for her children, amid all its perils. She began a new life in the rue du Temple in a house shared with her aunt, the widowed Mme de La Trousse, whose virtue, Bussy acknowledged, would make "the Précieuses blanch" (8.16.65), and "made herself the friend of four or five prudes with whom she goes everywhere." The society in which she charted her perilous course was not transformed and her own past was not dead. To everyone's surprise except her own, perhaps, when she first met in that society the man who had caused her husband's death, she fainted dead away.

CHAPTER 2

Distinction (1652-1663)

I *"Was I ever so pretty . . .?" (10.6.79)*

MME de Sévigné did not see herself as one of "nature's master-works," as novelists of her time characterized their fictional creations. The painting of her at forty by Claude Le Febvre, now in the Carnavalet fittingly opposite the Mignard portrait of her daughter, she judged a "countrified" image not apt to be viewed as "agreeable or tender" (8.7.75). More than the familiar full-face pastel by Nanteuil or the more reflective Versailles portrait of the Marquise a decade later, however, the Le Febvre canvas does animate for us the personality of the letter-writer in maturity.[1] Bussy's almost exactly contemporary prose portrait was sketched in much the same spirit of that student of Le Brun:

Mme de Sévigné has the finest complexion in the world, small but sparkling eyes, a flat mouth but of good color, a high forehead, a nose like nothing but itself—neither long nor short, square at the end—the lower part of the face like the tip of the nose, and all this, when taken to pieces not hand-some, is very agreeable all together. She has a fine shape without having a good air. Her leg is well made; her breast, hands, and arms, ill shaped. Her hair, very fine, and thick. She used to dance well and still has an agreeable voice.

So much for the appearance, Bussy concludes, and goes on to the wit, gaiety, and "dazzlement of prodigious vitality" that animate it. If "good air" is not captured in the 1665 portraits, it certainly is in earlier ones. Henri Beaubrun's of the thirteen-year-old Mlle de Chantal catches the sparkle of her distinctive eyes with their slightly different colored irises. The stunning full-length portrait of the young bride, at twenty, dressed in crimson with a garland of flowers in her hands, reflects the grace and scarcely contained animation which charmed society, catching the eye of more than one prose portraitist for whom beauty meant a captivating and distinctive grace, wit, and animation.

"I beseech you, interrupted Amilcas, be pleased to take the pains to give us a description of her beauty, wit, and humor. What you desire, replied Æmolius, is doubtless a harder task than you imagine, since there is something that is so delicate and so particular in the beauty and worth of the Princess Clarinta, that I think I shall not be able to find expressions proper enough to make you apprehend it."[2] In the emerging portrait that follows Mme de Sévigné had the pleasure of seeing herself transposed into the realm of fiction, in Part III of Mlle de Scudéry's fashionable novel *Clélie* (February 1657). Now, as nature's masterwork, her freshness is "as never seen but at the uprising of Aurora upon the finest roses of the spring" and her eyes "sky-blue and full of spirit" seem the very expression of her "freedom of air" and "lively imagination." Wide reading and wit, and more, enliven her conversation, which is "familiar, divertive and natural." "She speaks pertinently and well, nay sometimes she hath some natural and sprightly expressions that are infinitely taking; and though she be not of those immoveable beauties that are guilty of no action, yet do not the pretty gestures she uses proceed from any affectation, but are only the effects of her vivacity of spirit, liveliness of disposition, and divertive humor." All in all she seems "that very springtime of humor which becomes her so well, and which diverts herself while she diverts others."

At the apogee of a long gradation of qualities the widow Sévigné may have been most pleased to find the heroic virtue of "*gloire*," the elevation that gives merit to her charms. "Clarinta is also a lover of all excellent things, and all innocent pleasures, but she loves glory above her self, and what makes for her advantage, she hath found out the way, without being severe, savage, or solitary, to preserve the noblest reputation in the world, and that in a great Court, where all persons of worth have access to her and where she raises love in all those that are capable of it." Another woman sees differently, perhaps with a deeper sense of truth, what Bussy views as his cousin's mask of prudery.

Mlle de Scudéry adds one final trait, a revealing addition to the whole picture, the first of many tributes to Mme de Sévigné's writing as an extension of her conversation. "I had forgotten to tell

you that she writes as well as she speaks; that is, in the most
pleasant and gallant-like manner that may be. Nay, what is yet
further remarkable in this Princess, is, that her charms are so great,
and so unavoidable, that contrary to custom, she gains the hearts
of the ladies as well as men." Mme de Sévigné will not ask for more
in her letters to her daughter.

Entertained by the Duc de Lesdiguières in 1658, often by
Foucquet and others, Mme de Sévigné moved easily from the city's
society to the Court and presented her daughter there during the
first years of Louis's personal reign. She enjoyed the lavish
"Pleasures of the Enchanted Island" and Molière's triumphs
among them, and the epithet "Tartuffe," like so much of Molière's
language, was soon among her "sprightly expressions." It was no
surprise, then, for the Princess Clarinta to be transformed into
Sophronia in Somaize's *Grand Dictionnaire historique des
Précieuses* (1661), which is less a directory of the "new women"
society designated as *précieuses* than a *Who's Who* of women
reigning in salons because they had the wit and intelligence, charm
and magnetism to do so.[3] Sophronia had all that.

The merit of this person is equal to her name. Her wit is lively and playful,
and joy rather than melancholy is characteristic of her. It is at the same
time easy to judge that joy for her does not lead to love, for she only has
love for those of her own sex and is content to offer esteem to men—and
that she does not give easily.[4] She has the quickest mind in the world for
perceiving things and judging them. She is blond and of a fairness that
complements the beauty of her hair. The features of her face are fine, her
coloring even, and all that together composes one of the most agreeable
women of Athens [Paris]. But if her face catches the eye, her wit charms
the ear and engages all those who hear her or who read what she writes.
The most clever persons are proud to have her approbation. Ménandre
[Ménage] has sung the praises of this illustrious person in his verse, and
Chrisante [Chapelain] is also among those who visit her often. She loves
music and hates satire.

For society in the early 1660s, Mme de Sévigné's distinctive
personality, stylized in literary portraits, became a crystallized
distinction. Prose portraits in the last years of the 1650s were the
rage. Mme de Sévigné knew Mlle de Montpensier and had visited
her in exile at Saint-Fargeau. There a select company began the
fashion and, guided by her freedom of mind, humor, and talent,

composed a collection of fifty-nine portraits (*Divers portraits*, 1659). It contained a new, unsigned portrait of Mme de Sévigné, which was the first published writing of Mme de Lafayette, composed in 1658. When Mme de Sévigné happened upon it again years later, she was moved by its tribute of friendship, the "agreeable and tender" likeness she had not found in Le Febvre's portrait. "It has more worth than I do," she wrote Mme de Grignan, "but those who loved me sixteen years ago would have found it a good likeness" (12.1.75). First place is again given to animating wit, but underneath sparkling presence there are also special inner riches.

When you are animated in free conversation everything that you say has such charm and suits you so well that your words draw laughter and grace about you, and the brilliance of your wit gives such *éclat* to your complexion and to your eyes that although it seems that wit only touches the ears, it is certain that yours dazzles the eyes. . . . But I also want for you to see, Madame, that I know the solid qualities that you possess not less well than those agreeable ones that affect others. Your soul is great, noble, inclined to spend its wealth and incapable of lowering itself to the tasks of amassing it. You are sensitive to glory and ambition, no less so to pleasure. You seem born for them all, and they made only for you. . . . In short, joy is the true state of your soul, melancholy more out of keeping with you than with anyone else in the world. . . . You are naturally tender and passionate. . . .[5]

The portrait's final tribute is to a life very different from Mme de Lafayette's, to a gift of renewing love that would never allow Mme de Sévigné to feel as she did that "it is enough to be."[6] Mme de Sévigné felt, rather, as Molière's shepherdesses do, in the song that closes *La Princesse d'Elide*, that "A heart takes life/Only that day it knows love." Shortly after the publication of Mme de Lafayette's novel *The Princess of Cleves*, her friend quoted with approval belief that "the true measure of merit must be gauged by the extent and capacity that one has to love" (10.12.78). Ignoring correct attribution to Mlle de Scudéry, the keenly appreciative first English translator of Mme de Sévigné's *Letters* (anon., 1727) quotes the remark as "the noble maxim she has laid down." She greatly admired La Rochefoucauld's art, but only on rare and special occasions fashioned maxims herself. Her way to truth was different, leisurely and discursive reflection, always in dialogue, over

the years. But that one maxim she did "lay down." It is at the
center of the composite self-portrait that, in place of any formal
prose self-portrait reminiscent of the literary genre, is drawn over
the decades of letter-writing. It is the heart of self-knowledge, and
the coherence of a self-image already formed in the early 1660s,
that she will explore in response to her daughter's "mignards" but
not modify as her fundamental axiom.

On her prose portraits Mme de Sévigné retained a distance, a
half-amused smile at Sophronia or Princess Clarinta; the princess
in her life was by her own fashioning the young girl already playing
princess. Painting a moment made happy by her pleasure of
memory, she wrote to Mme de Grignan: "M. de Pomponne recalls
one day at my Uncle Sévigné's when you were a little girl. You were
behind a window with your brother, more beautiful than an angel,
he says; you said that you were a prisoner, that you were a princess
expelled from her father's house. Your brother was as beautiful as
you were. You were nine" (1.15.74). Beside the idealized portraits
of the mother similar family paintings had also been placed. After
the Abbé de Pomponne saw her in 1655 in an open carriage with
her beautiful children, he still remembered two years later a radiant
sight that seemed the very image of Latona with the young Apollo
and Diana.

No contemporary gave Mme de Sévigné the designation of
précieuse, though she was linked by friendship and tastes with
those women who most often were.[7] With the vivacity, lack of
affectation, natural and sprightly speech, evoked by the por-
traitists, no such caricature seems possible; nor is a "touch of
preciousness," in an opinion of the historian Nisard that had long
life, "the one superfluous ribbon in a simple and elegant toilette."
The spirit of Molière is too much there, and no one laughed more
heartily than she at his The Learned Ladies. Her uncle Renaud de
Sévigné and cousin Bussy were among the first to sneer at the
affectations of "the breed of young girls and women in Paris that
are called précieuses." She herself enjoyed the sarcasm, even at the
expense of the distinction of Mlle de Scudéry (3.20.71; 3.5.83),
"whose wit and penetration are limitless" (12.9.64; 9.25.80). It is
with her own sense of a special private irony, and a clear view of
her "most pleasant and gallant-like manner," that Mme de Sévigné
could always feel herself to have a bit of that folly of being pre-

cious, to indulge in the game with friends and to transform it with special meaning in letters to her daughter.

Since Mme de Sévigné wrote as she talked in society, the portraits tell us, and few persons in her society would not feel that the best familiar letters are simply extended conversation, new compliments from Costar in 1658 seem no more surprising than Somaize's bow to a distinction that was a matter of record. Preceptor to the children of her friend Mme de Lavardin, with whom she dined on Fridays and enjoyed conversation (*"lavardinage"*) in the company of the precious poet and librettist Benserade, Costar had given in to the vogue of publishing personal correspondence, not yet quite the thing to be done in some circles. He is, in the preface of his thick volume, at pains to defend himself against the vanity of following in the tradition of the "great Balzac and the agreeable Voiture." With his gift of the volume to Mme de Sévigné, he wrote that among so many letters "there is not one that is of the price of the slightest letters that escape from your pen every day, without meditation and effort, and which cost your hand more than your mind" (No. 46).

The vogue from which Costar profited is based on a long and noble tradition, extending back from the "great Balzac" to Pasquier and other Renaissance humanists and finally to Pliny and Cicero. It is a tradition, as Costar implies, to which Mme de Sévigné will owe nothing. But the tradition of the "agreeable Voiture" is another matter. The numerous first readers of his letters, published in a dozen editions during the decade after his death in 1648, would find repeated among compliments Voiture himself gave to his correspondents the same compliment given to Mme de Sevigne during that decade—"You write as you speak."

II *"A most agreeable and gallant-like manner"*

New peas and ripe artichokes, at least one bare bottom, even soiled linen find a place in Voiture's poetry. A tone of voice and smile managed it all, to the delight of Mme de Rambouillet, for whom the poet offered graceful performances of madrigal, rondeau, "metamorphosis," and riddle, among other verse entertainments. Prigs and prudes, like pedants, were not welcome, unless at their own expense, for fun-making from puerile practical

jokes to the most refined games of language was the order of the
day in this salon that set the tone for society during Mme de
Sévigné's adolescence.

Chapelain could deliver a reading of highly rhetorical epistles by
Balzac, intent upon shining as first letter-writer of the realm, issued
from his retreat near Angoulême. But the luster Mme de Rambouillet preferred in her salon was the kind of ironic compliment
that Voiture produced in pastiche of Balzac's epistolary style.[8] By
the end of the century it became the highest praise to say that a
letter-writer "possessed his Voiture"; no one in polite society failed
to discern a "Voiture." "You make me laugh," Mme de Sévigné
answered one such compliment, "when you believe that someone
could write like Voiture. I never tire of the grace (*agrément*) of his
style" (5.24.90).

Voiture's mode is irony, which covers a whole spectrum. Sarcasm shades into gentler persiflage, plays on inside-jokes and half-
hidden personal allusions, then shades again into a light self-
mockery of his own "performance." The lightest of performances,
for example in response to Mme de Rambouillet's request to have a
description of the house of the Duchesse de Savoie, contrive to
have things two ways—avoid tiresome set-pieces of description and
give delight in display of distinctive style.

Madame, for the love of you, I have seen Valentin with more attention
than I have given anything, and since you wish me to describe it to you, I
will do so as succinctly as possible. . . . Valentin, Madame, since Valentin it
is to be, is a house a quarter league from Turin situated in a meadow by the
Po. Upon arriving one first finds. . . . I hope to die if I know what one does
find first. I think it's a perron. No, no, it's a portico. I'm wrong, it is a
perron. My word, I don't know which it is. An hour ago I knew perfectly
well and now my memory fails me. When I return I will be better informed
and report.[9]

The elegant banter of the epistolary style on which Voiture set his
stamp is that elusive mixture of compliment and raillery, which is
the very definition of urbanity. Its "*agréments*" give the illusion of
a naturalness and ease beyond art.[10] But the performance depends
on a firm control of the moment and interlocutor that may trans-
late successfully into writing the improvisational movement and
suitable tone modulations of conversation. So reputed was he as a

master of "fine gallantry," of giving unique "price" to the distinction of ladies already much complimented, that he could indulge in a self-conscious display of "exposure" of that talent. To sting a lady who came upon it with jealousy, he could concoct, literally, a letter to "no one" about nothing at all.

There has never been so extraordinary or strange an attraction as that I have felt for you. I don't know who you are, and never in my life, to my knowledge, have I heard your name. Yet I assure you that I love you and that there has already been a day when you made me suffer. Without ever having seen your face I find it beautiful, and your wit seems agreeable to me although I have heard no sample of it. All your actions transport me, and I imagine in you an "I know not what" that makes me love an "I know not whom." Sometimes I imagine you blonde, sometimes brunette; tall, short; with an aquiline nose, with a turned-up nose. But in all the forms that I give you, you seem the most lovable thing in the world, and without knowing what sort of beauty you have I would swear it is the most lovable of all. If you know me so little and love me so much I thank love and the stars. But lest you should be mistaken, imagining me to be tall and blond, I will describe myself more or less. My height is two or three inches below average. I have a rather fine head with lots of gray hair, soft but bewildered eyes, and a rather foolish face. In recompense one of your friends will tell you that I am the best lover in the world and that no one can so faithfully as I love in five or six places at a time. If all that suits you, I will offer it on the first occasion.[11]

This elaborate joke, burlesque send-up of the fashionable description of beauty as an "I know not what" and pastiche of his own style, is less frequent among Voiture's letters than a more subdued and subtle play on the double vision of things for real correspondents on specific occasions. He could transform the debaucheries of Gaston d'Orléans into the feats of the old paladins or, with the best of Don Juans, flatter a country girl with a distinction of his own making. For Mme de Rambouillet or Mme de Sévigné, who took supreme pleasures in dance and masquerade, in scenic and poetic metamorphosis, ritualized distinction is both a form of life and a source of pleasure. Voiture's irony offers a simple pleasure to their imagination, but also a more complex and refined pleasure to the mind. Mme de Rambouillet may have been able to remain longer than Mme de Sévigné in the realms of masquerade. But for all the pride in her Savelli blood and the fine distinction that gave her a reign of unparalleled length over fashion, she was in no doubt about the fact of her mortality. As Arthénice, she took special pleasures in seeing her daughters, Julie and Angélique-Clarice d'Angennes (the first Mme de Grignan) transformed into goddesses by Voiture, just as Latona (Mme de Sévigné) relived in memory the first pleasures of seeing her daughter dancing in the settings of Benserade's mythological and allegorical court ballets.[12] For the mind, the unforgotten reality continues to play against the fiction: as mothers and women both knew that this ritualized and perfect beauty was a special—and momentary—triumph of art.

The entire lexicon of Petrarchan love language is incorporated into Voiture's gallantry. But in his letters, as in his poetry, that imagery often contrasts with or is undercut by the cacophony of a low word or sexually sly allusion. The mixture of tones in his collected letters and his breaking of textures in individual letters have parallels in Mme de Sévigné's letters, as they do in Bussy's. So does his pleasure with brevity and a quick pace—an accumulation of quickening verbs, for example, or the rapid donning and doffing of what thereby becomes a caricatural pastoral or romanesque mask. These devices of style among others create in Voiture's letters the impression of a freedom of ever inventive language and of life in constant readaptation. The impression delighted both La Fontaine and Mme de Sévigné, who like the poet of the fables gives in her writing a special sense of the openness, variety, and fullness of living.

The poet Voiture, who assumes absence as the domain of his art and seeks to touch others by it in his letters, expresses melancholy in solitude with a tenderness at moments that Mme de Sévigné may have heard anew after separation from her daughter.

Seeing a bright winter sunrise over the mountains, Voiture sits beside the Rhône, and the beauty of the scene makes his mind turn only to the beloved he has left behind. Each of his sighs seems a part of his soul leaving his body; each sigh, he insists, "is true," just as Mme de Sévigné will press upon her daughter that insistent reality of revery. From Rome he wrote that the greatest art, the beauty of gardens in spring or of ruins, are no consolation for absence, and concludes with a simile that Mme de Sévigné maintains over years of letters to Mme de Grignan. "To be truthful you are like health. I never know your price so well as when I have lost you. You are the most precious thing in the world and all the delights of this earth are bitter and disagreeable without you." From Amiens he confessed: "I saw His Majesty play at cards after dinner today and am no more gay. I go regularly three times a week on fox-hunts but find no great joy in them, although there are always a hundred dogs and a hundred horns making a frightful din. The greatest pleasures of the greatest king on earth do not divert me, and the delights of the Court are indifferent to me when I do not see you."[13] Mme de Sévigné speaks no differently of the pleasures of Paris and the Court after first separation from her daughter.

Before all else was the simple joy of reading Voiture, heightened in time by always pleasant memories of the Rambouillet salon, whose prestige and spirit must have reached and touched Mlle de Chantal before they became a part of her life. As it would have appeared in Mme de Rambouillet's drawingroom, it seems to Mme de Sévigné an outrage that the Chevalier de Méré should pedantically criticize, in his "dog of a style," the "free, playful, charming wit of Voiture" (11.24.79). But, she reflected, as those around Arthénice might have, that "there are certain things one never understands when one does not understand them at first. Certain inflexible and grumpy minds cannot be made to enter into the charm and the ease of the ballets of Benserade or the fables of La Fontaine" (5.14.86). With pride in taste worthy of the Rambouillets she first and last understood those qualities.

In the 129 extant letters that give a surprisingly rich view of Mme de Sévigné before the age of forty-five, the world of Voiture's letters often seems near. Compliment is piled upon compliment, with Lenet and Montreuil, Scarron, Costar and Chapelain, Ménage and Bussy. Verses by Voiture ornament letters to her, and in turn she tries her own hand at improvising similar lines of her own. Madrigals are sent to amuse her, as is the eleventh of Pascal's *Provincial Letters*, thought "very fine" but given in her letter less attention than the madrigals (9.12.56).

First letters are usually short, the shortest a playful one-word note to Lenet. The Marquise at first cultivated brevity, to strike the tone of a crisp urbanity, which predominates in her early letters and gives them the mark of her own style. The most serious matters, civil war and financial distress, as already seen, modulated by this tone all lose their sting, at least until 1661. But "an hour of con-

versation is better than fifty letters,'' she declared to Lenet
(3.25.49), and that attitude underlies all her early letters. Necessary,
of course, since they effect action and prolong conversation when
both are physically impossible, letters also participate in the
pleasures of conversation. Like urbane conversation, her letters at
first withhold as much as they give; feeling is masked behind conventional banter and flattering turns of phrase. They take joy in
display of wit unencumbered by extended narration, formal
description, or sustained analysis. Such conversation with an
interlocutor as notoriously sharp-tongued as Ménage could be an
adventure, and so was correspondence with him.

The coquetry Mme de Sévigné assumes with Ménage is by turns
playfully reproachful, in response for example to the "lover's"
pouting over his "loved one's" departures, then cajoling and
bluntly mocking. "If Montreuil weren't twelve times as scatter-
brained as a may-bug you would have seen that I have not insulted
you," she wrote to Ménage, offended over not being collected for a
drive, adding bluntly that he might simply have looked at the
weather (No. 27, 1654?). In one note she could manage to comment on his style; thank him for a favor; solicit another; and still
keep the balance-sheet of their friendship to her own credit. The
manner that makes all this work, in a letter really *about* business of
her estate of Buron, had to learn nothing from the popular
"secretaries" that offered ladies in need "model" letters for such
moments nor to fear lapses into their clichés.[14]

Your note was the prettiest in the world. That's the way I advise you to
write them. I am delighted that my little eyes have made such illustrious
conquests and honored indeed if they brought disorder to so high a place as
the Council of State. But I fear that is only half the story. In any case, I am
happy with the esteem, which I beg you to guard for me since you won it.
As for M. de Noirmoutier, I will take charge, for he is on his way to gain
admission herein, and it is here that I await him to gain his heart. After all,
you have the glory of my being more fond of yours than all others. And
whatever indignity I had to undergo during the time I took to gain it, I am
consoled when I think of its worth. (No. 24, 1653?)

To gain a heart and esteem, and good press (obviously a first
concern here), is a tricky affair when notes combine cajoling
gratitude, business, and a taunting coquetry purposely enigmatic

about "rivals" (No. 25, 1654?). Mme de Lafayette, early on cast as a "rival" by a noncommittal Marquise (No. 20), joked with Ménage about "great revolutions in the empire of Love" (2.20.57), which were in fact not long in coming. From 1657 on there is no regular exchange. But during the troubles of 1661 Mme de Sévigné found a new mixture of prudence, pride, and politics for notes enlisting his aid (Nos. 51, 53-55).

Twenty years after the first prickly exchanges, when Ménage broke long silence with a new poetic tribute, Mme de Sévigné closes correspondence with him on a different note. The final tone is a delicate apology for a balance-sheet of friendship in the past too easily calculated in her own favor.

Your memento gave me real joy and made me recall all the agreement of our old friendship. Your verses brought back my youth, and I would indeed like to know why so irreparable a loss has not made me sad. . . . For the honor of your verse I should have better merited that honor you do me. Such as I have been, and am now, I shall never forget your true and solid friendship and will be all my life the most grateful, and the oldest of your humble servants. (6.23.73)

The Marquise de Sévigné, as she signed her note, was writing from Aix and joyful reunion with her daughter. After the emotional drama and drain of 1671-72, she both regretted the melodrama she had forced Ménage to play and through a glow of nostalgia chose to smile at a more carefree past.

No letters of the early correspondence are more worthy of Voiture than those addressed to the Grande Mademoiselle or to others about her, when the grand opera of her love for Lauzun, brought to its ill-fated conclusion, became a *cause célèbre* and instantly a sentimental novel, rewritten in the gossip and letters of every woman of her society. The one extant letter addressed to Her Royal Highness, from Les Rochers (10.30.56), is the mixture of verse and prose made popular by the poet Malleville, no less skill-fully combined than in similar letters Bussy sent to his cousin. Initial verses and prose deliberately prolong pleasures of conversation she had had at Saint-Fargeau, then are followed by an amusing mock-heroic narrative of a provincial outing with a bit of Breton folklore. Told in a bantering "fairy-tale" tone that does little credit to its power, the folklore seems to have caught the imagination of

Mademoiselle, who had a report drawn on the "legend of the Montfort duck." The letter may have come to be known as the "Montfort letter," as both Voiture's and later Mme de Sévigné's own letters came sometimes to be known by titles in a select society.

Mlle de Montpensier is among the few women untouched by Bussy's satire, and much about her, independence of mind and spirit, taste and enjoyment of fine writing, must have been admired by both Bussy and Mme de Sévigné. Especially imposing was her extraordinary devotion to her own idea of her *gloire*. If that devotion could be blind, as it seems in the extravagant love affair that amounted to a physical "appropriation" of Lauzun, the willful blindness completed the portrait of the Corneillian heroine that her uniquely high rank and active role in the Fronde had already suggested to the imaginations of her contemporaries. Astonished by news that the greatest heiress in France was about to enter into the greatest misalliance, Mme de Sévigné sought to recreate for her cousin Philippe-Emmanuel in Lyons a sense of the astonishment that had set the whole Court on its ear. Playing with the salon game of the riddle, as she had with Grignan (12.10.70), she first entertains Coulanges by an exuberant performance that has remained her most famous "display letter."

I am going to tell you a thing that is the most astonishing, the most surprising, the most marvellous, the most miraculous, the most supreme, the most dizzying, the most unheard, the most singular, the most extraordinary, the most incredible, the most unforeseen, the greatest and the smallest, the rarest and most common, the most public and until today the most secret, the most brilliant, the most envied—in short a thing known only once in past centuries—and that not really the same—a thing that we cannot believe in Paris (how could it be believed in Lyons?)—a thing which makes everyone cry mercy—a thing that is the crowning joy of Mme de Rohan and Mme de Hauterive[15]—a thing finally that will be done Sunday and that those who see will not believe—a thing that will be done Sunday and perhaps will not be finished Monday. I cannot make myself tell you what. Guess. I'll give you three guesses. Give up? Very well, then, I must tell you. Lauzun is to be married Sunday, at the Louvre, to——guess whom? I'll give you four guesses, ten, a hundred! Mme de Coulanges may well say, "That's a hard one. It is Mlle de La Vallière." Not at all, Madame. "Then it's Mlle de Retz." Not at all, you've been in the country. "Certainly, how stupid," you say, "it's Mlle Colbert." You're getting colder. "Then it's surely Mlle de Créquy."[16] You're really off. You must finally be told—he is marrying Sunday, at the Louvre, with the King's leave, Mlle, Mlle de, Mlle—guess her name. He is marrying Mlle, my word! My sworn word! Mlle, the Grande Mlle, daughter of the late Monsieur, granddaughter of Henri IV, Mlle d'Eu, Mlle de Dombes, Mlle de Montpensier, Mlle d'Orléans; Mlle the King's cousin, Mlle destined for a throne, Mlle the only worthy match for Monsieur. There is a fine subject for discourse. If you cry out, are beside yourself, say we have lied, declare us false, say that you're mocked, that this is fine raillery, a poor joke, if finally you insult us, you should. We did just the same ourselves. (12.15.70)

Four days later, when the King's opposition ended the dream, Mme de Sévigné's flurry gives way to more sober diversion. She becomes an entirely detached spectator of a drama that just verges on comedy. "As for Mlle, in keeping with her humor, she bursts into tears, exclamations, violent grief, excessive lamentations, and the entire day she kept to her bed, swallowing nothing but bouillons. A fine dream, a fine subject for a novel or tragedy, but especially a fine subject for meditation and eternal conversation. That is what we do day and night, morning and evening, ceaselessly and endlessly; we hope that you are doing the same" (12.19.70). Another week brings another modification; the game continues, the tone remains amused, but esteem and personal feeling begin to be felt. "You know now the romanesque history of Mlle and M. de Lauzun. It is a fit subject for a tragedy with all the rules of the theater. We drew up the acts and scenes the other day. . . . Lauzun played his role to perfection. . . . Mlle also did very well indeed. She wept well. She returned today to do her duties at the Louvre, where she receives everyone. There is the end" (12.24.70).

It was not quite the end. Moved finally by the woman to whom she offered the compliment of quoting Corneille's *Polyeucte* one day and consolation the next, Mme de Sévigné recounted the whole sequence once more. Abandoning earlier stylization, her final and finest letter on the affair expresses affection and sympathy, that expression which softens her last letter to Ménage and is characteristic of the new distinction of some of the finest of her mature letters of the 1670s. After admiring and emulating heroic stifling of emotion, she enters into it from her own deeper feeling that "the true measure of merit must be gauged by the extent and capacity that one has to love." The impending drama of separation and loss in her own life, she admits, is too real for her not to do so, not to feel sympathy or to withhold compassion from others who feel that drama. "The next day, which was Friday, I went to visit her and found her on her bed. She redoubled her cries when she saw me, called out to me, embraced me, wet me with her tears. She said, 'Alas, do you remember what you said to me yesterday? O cruel prudence! O prudence!' Her crying made me cry. I returned twice more. She is very distressed and has treated me always as a person who could feel it. She has not been wrong. I have rediscovered feelings one scarcely feels for persons of such rank. All this is between us, and Mme de Coulanges, for you know that this conversation would be entirely ridiculous to some persons" (12.31.70).

Ridiculous it would have seemed to Mme de Montespan. In her memoirs, fabricated but often incisive, the acerbic "Mortemart wit" reduced Mademoiselle to a grotesquely ridiculous figure. "When one has been pretty, one imagines that one is still so, and will forever remain so. Plastered up and powdered, consumed by passion and, above all blinded by vanity, she fancied that Nature had to obey princes and that, to favor her, Time would stay its flight."[17] That sarcasm could not be further from Mme de Sévigné's last response or, it seems, her natural wit. Although she frankly enjoys sarcasm and is capable of cruelty, in unsentimental and lucid detachment, her wit never indulges long in the brittle and ruthlessly reductive ridicule of the Mortemarts (which suggested the "Guermantes wit" to Proust's imagination).

Closer in spirit to the verbal inventiveness of Voiture, and exalting in that freedom, Mme de Sévigné's is more the "Coulanges wit" whose pleasures her favorite cousin keeps bright. His "follies and visions make me faint with laughter" (11.29.84); "gaiety is a great part of his merit" (9.18.89). The festive letter to him in which the Marquise describes her pitching in during the haying at Les Rochers (7.22.71) may in fact be someone else's good story (Duchêne, I, 1129-30), a pastiche amplifying the same scene recounted for her daughter in the spirit of letters to Coulanges. But that spirit remains. Almost to her last letter, his easily turned songs and compliments delight her and even inspire a satirical song or two to accompany her laughter. "The style one has when writing to him is like joy and health" (11.15.84).

Gaiety, joy, and health have always seemed in her turn a great part of the letter-writer's "merit." Yet there is in her letters, even before her daughter's departure, an understanding of the reality of human suffering. That understanding and a sense of shared humanity fostered by it are there increasingly behind the smile, creating the nuances of Mme de Sévigné's letters that Charles Péguy called her characteristic "regard of half-amused commiseration before human weakness."[18] No spectacle did more to fix its permanent presence than events of 1661-64 that swept Foucquet to life imprisonment.

CHAPTER 3

Trials (1654-1670)

I   *Foucquet*

IT was not only La Fontaine who wept for the silence of the
nymphs of Vaux, and his unfinished "Dream of Vaux" is not its
only transformation into art. The Château and grounds, adorned
by fountains of a magnificence unknown in France, by spacious
lawns, by groves graced by the highest aristocracy and most celebrated persons in France were an ideal setting for elegant diversion,
which Molière among others provided with his light comedy *The
Bores* (*Les Fâcheux*). Vaux was an easy subject for Mlle de Scudéry,
who extolled its master Cléomire and described in her fiction the
paintings done for him by Méléandre (Le Brun). A place of en-
chantment, of idealized beauty and gallantry, it was as evanescent a
dream as any idealization the Princess Clarinta knew: in 1661 the
Château was padlocked to await legal inventory and its master
became the subject of the greatest criminal trial of seventeenth-
century France.

At the mercy of a chaotic financial empire, and of a minister,
Mazarin, who demanded ready cash rather than accountability,
Foucquet's speculations enmeshed him in a nightmare of intrigue,
contingency plans in case of rapid fall from favor, growing debt
and soaring envy. When, after Mazarin's death, he was called to
full legal accountability, the personal fortune and financial manip-
ulations that had seen the royal treasury through more than one
crisis in the 1650s could not be set in order. The court of special
jurisdiction was manned by judges unfavorable to him. Foucquet's
trial was in fact Mazarin's trial.[1] And some 1,200 letters from
Mazarin, Foucquet charged, had disappeared.

Foucquet's arrest on September 5, 1661, and charges against him
of financial collusion and treason, incriminated many who had

contracted debts to him or served him. His closest agents fled the country. His secretary Pellisson, to Mme de Sévigné the "most honest of honest men" (No. 53, October 1661), received her consolation at the beginning of lengthy imprisonment. Her high praise was justified in 1662 by his sober and powerfully argued defense of Foucquet, widely circulated and praised by Voltaire as worthy of the best of Cicero. Compromised also were great ladies, whose real or elusive favors combined in letters with legitimate business had found their way into his famous strongbox. They remained among personal papers confiscated irregularly and withheld from his defense attorneys.

Foucquet's prolonged trial triggered a war of polemics and galvanized public opinion to the extent that it invites comparison with the Dreyfus affair that shook French society during the last years of the nineteenth century. In spring 1662, Colbert ordered that any person writing in favor of the accused would be prosecuted. But virulent attacks on Colbert and pleas for Foucquet continued to appear anonymously. The most violent, *Innocence Persecuted*, emanated from the Jansenist salon of Mme du Plessis-Guénégaud, a friend Mme de Sévigné sought out during tense moments of the trial (12.9.64).[2]

For La Fontaine, spared serious penalty for public loyalty to his former patron, the whole spectacle of the abuses of the machinery of justice became an essential part of the experience crystallizing the vision of injustices of power that chills readers of the first collection of fables (1668).[3] For Mme de Sévigné the experience was a similarly powerful one.

Among letters kept by Foucquet were some in which Mme de Sévigné had, it seems, negotiated affairs of her cousin La Trousse. The man whose courtship is reflected enigmatically in her early letters with Bussy may never have gained from her favors so easily collected from many others. One will now never know. By an act of gallantry worthy of the first gentleman of the realm, Louis XIV destroyed the evidence of Foucquet's strongbox. What is certain is that panic struck Mme de Sévigné. She knew too well the fragility of reputations at moments when scandal reigns. Spurious letters supposedly copied from those in the strongbox were quick to pass from hand to hand.

Mme de Sévigné's distinguished friend, Arnauld de Pomponne,

sometime ambassador and minister of the crown, first warned her of danger. Suspected as an intermediary between Foucquet and the Jansenists and exiled, Pomponne shared danger with her. In October when it seemed she "heard nothing but Foucquet" (10.9.61), aid was solicited from both Ménage and Chapelain. After a clumsy first "defense," Chapelain put her mind to rest temporarily (No. 56).

When the first panic of "exposure" subsided, Mme de Sévigné's emotions remained high and her nerves taut at the mention of Foucquet. After seeing the King turn his back on repeated pleas by his mother and wife (11.20.64), personal fear gave way to concern for the prisoner and pity for his dispersed family. Never would she agree with Chapelain that Foucquet was a "miserable personage," guilty of criminal blindness in regard to friends (No. 57). It was to the more sympathetic Pomponne that she sent her sixteen dispatches on Foucquet's fate between mid-November 1664 and spring 1666.

Mme de Sévigné's famous letters on Foucquet's trial are not reportage based on direct observation of events. The sessions held at the Arsenal, almost daily from November 14 through December 4, 1664, were closed. She and others tried to convey continued concern indirectly. Going masked to a house near the Arsenal, she waited at a window for a guard to direct Foucquet's attention to her, and when "his smiling face" acknowledged her presence, she was intensely moved. "When I saw him my legs trembled and my heart beat so hard that I could not bear it. If you knew how unfortunate one is to have a heart like mine, you would pity me. But knowing you as I do, I know that you are no less affected" (11.27.64). On court proceedings she had the best of informants, her kinsman d'Ormesson, who gains in the whole affair the stature of the "Zola" of the trial. Charged in pretrial with the onerous task of judge-advocate, under the watchful eye of the presiding magistrate, Chancellor Séguier, he stood constantly for the endangered rights of the accused. His five-day summation preserved whatever justice was salvaged from this political trial that had prejudged Foucquet guilty and, as he knew, condemned him to death.

Traditionally praised as the triumph of a gift for observation, Mme de Sévigné's letters on the trial are rather the achievement of a keen imagination and of an art fully given to its service. The powerful evocation of reality her "coverage" conveys is a special reality, different from the coverage of other letter-writers, Condé's for the Queen of Poland or Patin's, and from the detachment of d'Ormesson's journal. Her letters are human documents, and her gaze never for long leaves the face and image of Foucquet. Scenes she paints around Foucquet on trial are full and vivid, much like pictures of all-absorbing conspiracy in civil war Retz evokes in his *Mémoires*. But they are smaller canvases, to be viewed by one man who could fill out details, not historical frescoes meant for display.

In her first letter, Mme de Sévigné reflects on appropriate style for the letter-account (*relation*) she proposes to write each evening and to dispatch as a "letter-gazette" twice weekly. "Adieu, I feel the urge to chat coming, and I don't want to give in to it; the style of accounts should be short" (11.17.64). She tries to observe this "rule." Still she takes time for compliments to Pomponne, to "our dear solitary" (his father, Arnauld d'Andilly), to their "incomparable neighbor," Mme Du Plessis, in her "enchanted palace"; news of the Paris Arnaulds, Louis and the Queen, of the army and finances. As most often when she wishes to be brief, and the letter curbs her usual conversational bent, the famous phrase "I must tell you . . ." breaks in. Naturally so, since she is as at ease in her letters to Pomponne as she will be in conversation with him after the trial. Fortunately, too, since the real background of her letters is less the courtroom than her own busy life, taken over more and more by events and finally immobilized by tensions of expectation. This time while waiting for Act V to come she declares twice that "to live the life we are living is not to live" (12.5.64). She lives rather than speculates at a distance on the suspense of a well-made tragedy.

The busy life that breaks into the letters' chronicle of the trial is almost always relegated to their openings and closings, coloring events and setting tone. Sometimes the coloring is somber, as in her account of a visit to the Visitation convent in the rue Saint-Antoine. She found great concern there for Foucquet and sees Pomponne's aunt at Mass "as though in ecstasy" (11.21.64). Against this consoling religion, she orchestrates for Pomponne the macabre comedy played by the consciences of some of Foucquet's aging judges, troubled by recurrent omens and whispers of "God's judgment."

In a masterful letter (11.24.64), Mme de Sévigné recounts the visit to the Visitation convent of the aged Chancellor Séguier, who

sought relief there in his illness by visiting the relics of Saint Francis
and from them the balm of "a spark of the love of God that consumed the Saint." Using multiple installments of the letter-gazette
subtly, she contrasts in one part Séguier's public presence at the
trial, where he visibly obeys Colbert, with this semiprivate devotion. Incomprehension is her response. "If you ask me now what I
think of it, I will tell you that I don't know, that I don't understand
it, and that I cannot imagine what use this comedy is."

Having repressed Rabutin wit, Mme de Sévigné is delighted to
hear something like it when Pomponne interprets Séguier's con-
duct. "I am in despair that it wasn't I who said 'it is the metamorphosis of Pierrot into Tartuffe.' That is so right that if I had as
much wit as you say I do, I would surely have found it at the tip of
my pen" (12.1.64). The phrase seems so right because it has the
ring of Molière. It focuses the ridicule of the situation, Seguier's
lack of competence in financial matters, which she herself constantly notes with no concession in this privacy to her friendship
with his daughter, the Duchesse de Verneuil. She did not find it at
the tip of her pen because the character-portrait of Séguier that
emerges from her letters, far different from the idealized dignity
familiar from Le Brun's portrait, is richer than this caricature. As
the seventy-six-year-old Chancellor waxes ominously and wanes
ridiculously, the Séguier of her letters is closer to a character in
Balzac's human comedy.

The letters that follow the fourteen sessions of the trial she
covered (Nos. 59-65), like those reporting final judgment, are quite
similar, even with their garlands of different but surprisingly
integrated digressions. The central focus of each, most often the
center or body literally, is the trial. The recurrent phrase, in some
variation present in each, is "He responded marvellously." Focus
is thus from the first on performance or presence. Dialogue prevails, giving immediacy and direct illustration of Foucquet's self-
control, his symbolic protests of the court's jurisdiction, his
dignity as he maintains it in misfortune. Not alone in the spotlight,
he shares it with Séguier, who challenges constantly and in a
manner that seems beneath the high dignity of his own position.
Charges named by the letter-writer each day, sometimes not quite
accurately, are obviously less important to her than this symbolic
man-to-man combat.

In the first letter, Séguier begins combat with the charge that Foucquet's failure to recognize the court's jurisdiction is an affront to the King. Foucquet parries by putting Séguier himself on trial. To Foucquet goes the victory, of gesture if not in fact, and that for the Marquise is quite enough. She re-orders d'Ormesson's account[4] to give it full force of dramatic focus. Séguier had challenged that "although you do not recognize the court, you respond to it, you present petitions to it, and are there on the stand." Foucquet's response: "It is true, Monsieur, that I am here. But I am not here by my will. There is a power to which one must answer, and it is a mortification that God makes me suffer and that I receive from his hand. I might perhaps have been spared it after the services I have given and the charges I have honorably held." "Those who love M. Foucquet find his tranquility admirable. I am among them," Mme de Sévigné concluded, and added acidly: "Others say it is an affectation. There's the way of the world!" (11.20.64).

As in the beginning, so at the end. Ordered by the King to get on with it all, and forced to rise early, Séguier drifts off during a lengthy reading of charges. Justice sleeps, and Mme de Sévigné savors the scene. Foucquet "answered very well, but he became confused over certain dates, which would have embarrassed him if others had been on their toes and wide awake. But rather than that, the Chancellor dozed peacefully. Everyone looked at one another, and I think that our poor friend would have laughed, had he dared" (11.26.64).

As the trial neared conclusion, Judge Nesmond died, of the same disease afflicting Séguier, and before death asked forgiveness of Foucquet's family for his part in the trial. It was not the first omen reported or the last to prey on the Chancellor's mind. Remarkably free herself from superstition, Mme de Sévigné observed caustically: "If that gives him the sentiments of a man who is going to appear before God, it would be something, but it is to be feared that it will be said of him as of Argant [in Tasso's *Jerusalem Delivered*] he dies as he lived" (12.2.64).

The figure of dignity before final judgment that Foucquet assumes by contrast in Mme de Sévigné's last letters, which enshrine his image (Nos. 70-71), achieves final victory. For her the trial is won in the last session that dealt with the charge of treason. Foucquet admits that contingency plans formed as precaution but never implemented were the creation of an unwell mind. D'Ormesson recommends that the charge be dropped, but it takes a louder tone to reach Séguier. Rising to climactic indignation, and to heroic stature in Mme de Sévigné's letter (12.4.64), Foucquet turns the charge of treason against Séguier, who in the last days of the Paris Fronde had supported the rebel princes. That Séguier should have been pardoned is enough. That he should be judging a man who remained faithful to his King is the final absurdity brought to bear by the letter-writer, as chilling as any capricious play of power in the first books of La Fontaine's fables.

To get Foucquet's final charge just right, Mme de Sévigné repeats and amplifies it. In first form, in the fine letter recounting the trial's last day, it is stark and hits the mark squarely. "M. Foucquet responded: 'Monsieur, at all times, and even in peril of my life, I have never abandoned the person of the King, and in those days you were, Sir, the head of the council of his enemies, and your family lent passage to the army of his enemies.' The Chancellor felt the blow." Amplification adds the laughter of poetic justice. "The Chancellor did not know what to do with himself, and all the judges were sorely tempted to laugh . . ." (12.9.64).

The final absurdity of the trial is an indirect indictment of Louis XIV and, of course, Colbert, given the scornful code name "Tiny" (*Petit*). Criticism of the King runs implicitly through the letters and surfaces in a revealing anecdote, underscoring both the frivolity of the world, when such important matters are at hand, and cruelty all of a piece with Louis's treatment of Foucquet. "One morning the King said to the Maréchal de Gramont: 'M. le Maréchal, I pray you read this little madrigal, and see whether you have ever seen one that is so impertinent. Since it has become known that I like verse, I am brought all sorts of it.' The Maréchal, after reading it, said to the King: 'Sire, Your Majesty judges all things divinely. That is truly the most stupid and silly madrigal that I have ever seen.' The King began to laugh and said to him: 'Is it not true that the author is a fop?' 'Sire, there's no other word for it.' 'Good,' said the King, 'I am delighted that you have spoken so plainly. I wrote it.' 'Ah, Sire, what perfidy! Please give it back! I read it so quickly!' 'No, M. le Maréchal, first responses are always the most natural' " (12.1.64).

The letter-writer does not share the laughter. "The King laughed greatly at this folly, and everyone finds it the cruelest little trick that could be played on an old courtier. For my part, since I always like to reflect, I would wish that the King might reflect on this himself and judge how far he is from always knowing the truth." For Colbert (who into the bargain reduces interest rates, she complains), Mme de Sévigné always has the scorn implicit in the "Petit" of her letters on the trial. For the final absurdity of the King's power, she finds resignation with age and the flowering of his reign. But from the trial on there is a real fear of the King and a critical stance that keep her wary and free from the blindness of total admiration.

Mme de Sévigné's letters on the Foucquet trial and its aftermath are the writing of an artist fully in control of her art. Without surrendering anything of her own personality, indeed by using her personal style to enhance the kind of letter she defines for herself, she conveys the fullness of her view of the events and the strength of her personal vision of their human significance. Devotion to friends, both Foucquet and Pomponne, transforms style from free-playing display to a controlled expression of emotion. For the first time, too, letter-writing is spoken of as "consolation" (11.24.64), not just as prolonged conversation. Consolation for absence, certainly, but it is also a writer's consolation, the taming of the "heart like mine" through writing with all its devices—anecdotes, news, compliments, wit, narrations—that will be the consolation and the redemption through writing sought in the letters written to her absent daughter.

II *Bussy*

In 1680 Bussy wrote his cousin that some of his writings about to be sent to the King contained letters from her, "from 1673 to the end of 1675, the three years of our lives in which you wrote to me most often and the best letters" (12.28.80). This "third party," whom Bussy himself called "the delight and terror of the world," alarmed her. "Do you think the letters can be admired?" she replied, suggesting how little she had thought herself a "published author." "All I hope is that you have touched them up. Don't you believe that my style, filled as it always is with affection, might be misinterpreted? I have never seen letters of this sort that could not be, by a third party, and that would do great injustice to the truth and innocence of our old friendship" (1.12.81). Bussy reassured her with a handsome refusal. "I have not touched your letters, Madame; Le Brun would not retouch a Titian, where that great man left some negligence. Lesser talents are those to be revised and corrected" (1.17.81).

This mellowness is far from typical. Early letters especially are separated by considerable gaps of time caused by quarrels. But the cousins' exchange of letters, which runs like a spine through Mme de Sévigné's correspondence, reflects her development and a mastery of expression that Bussy long before 1681 had generously praised. Typically still in 1681, it is Bussy who judges in matters of style; Mme de Sévigné, judged, more or less willingly. In the beginning, exchanges with Bussy-"Le Brun" were not at all between equals, and Mme de Sévigné was criticized, on trial quite willingly. After the quarrel over Bussy's portrait of her in 1665, letters are most often characterized as "trials" (*procès*). The vexatious litigants make those letters lively courtrooms. With flamboyant combativeness, "combat at arms" is through 1681 the second metaphor both sustain to describe their correspondence.

Early letters display striking similarity and freedom of language. "It seems to me that we bring out the best in each other and say things that we would not elsewhere," Bussy wrote, reflecting on early years of friendship. They needed only to talk, he recalled, "to say everything" (9.7.68). Together, half-spoken exchanges, a glint of the eye, a smile often sufficed for understanding. Separated, Mme de Sévigné joked, she knew by her Rabutin blood when he was bled and had herself no need for the surgeon. Letters from his campaigns were enthusiastically awaited. With the Sévignés often, Bussy introduced his young cousin to the Hôtel de Richelieu, where the pleasures of the Rambouillets continued. He wrote to her in Brittany, and in her widowhood offered diversion, advice, and affectionate concern. "I say that you were a good fortune for your husband and would have been for a greater lord and a man of greater merit," he wrote later, echoing that concern (12.8.68).

Small wonder with Bussy in the family that Méré's codification of society's "rules" seemed lifeless and pedantic to Mme de Sévigné. Her eighteen-year-old cousin had dazzled her with the reality, when she was eight and he attended the family council that determined her future. The young captain possessed all the swagger, the elegance and articulateness, that put him with La Feuillade, Candale, and Lauzun, the tone setters and darlings of Regency society. His description of Mme de Sévigné's father's "sparkle" reflected his own. Readings from Voiture mirrored his own style. And Mme de Sévigné imitated his style, the most important and lasting direct influence on her own epistolary style. "Under cover of writing like a little Cicero, you believe yourself permitted to mock" (11.25.55), she rejoined in his own tone, the *Rabutinage* defined as family wit but not described by Littré's dictionary. Even in the most strained moments she confessed that "everything you write is agreeable, and if I were to wish the loss of something, or be indifferent to it, it would not be one of your letters" (1.7.69).

Understanding and judgment, like taste and temperament, tightened bonds. Bussy was as lucid on unrequited love as in analysis of self-interest. "Her extreme passion for me," he wrote of an early romance, "which should have augmented my own left me only with gratitude. I saw indeed that I was not being fair, but what could I do: it pleased love to order it thus." "He has said it all," Bussy's biographer concludes,[5] and certainly his lucidity and fatalism said much to Mme de Sévigné in marriage and widowhood, as did his *Maxims of Love* (reportedly read aloud by Louis XIV to his mistress Mlle de La Vallière). Among their "questions of love" distilled from that experience of inequality in love is one she may have reached more than once and accepted as axiomatic: "To know why of two lovers who love one another there is always one who loves more than the other."[6]

Mme de Sévigné's judgments of Foucquet's trials and celebration of his triumphs derived from a feudal and aesthetic sense of order of which Bussy was the very embodiment. With all the feudal aristocrat's tenacity he held onto rights of self-determination, of actions and gestures in accordance with his own concept of dignity, depending on courage, victory, and *gloire*. Restless under any restraints, mistrusting the new brand of government functionaries, he smarted with injustice over royal disfavor and exile to his Burgundian estate in the wake of his satirical *Amorous History of the Gauls*. Birth and feeling are the criteria both cousins share in

judging individuals. In his letters and hers it is the innate quality—
nobility, beauty, courage, wit that is made to tell. In life in exile, as
in historical narrative that might settle accounts properly with his
King, Bussy sought a triumph of pure style, through elegant simplicity and frankness that would illustrate a "natural love of
truth," his own truths. His rule in all things, letters and conversation certainly, was just that, his own truth, that sacred naturalness
of his caste. "Propriety in naturalness" was the rule; the motto,
"Preserve the natural,\ it alone gives worth."[7]

Before all else in his prose Bussy sought concision. In his historical writing narrative must be short and concise, for it is tiresome
if not, "however fine the events it treats" (2.14.78), as Mme de
Sévigné also said to Pomponne in 1664. His *Amorous History*
stings the more sharply for this effort. It is impossible to read the
crisp sentences on Mme d'Olonne's "honorable treaties," for
example, without thinking of Voltaire's *Candide* and the ironic
presentation of its Marquise de Parolignac.[8] Our most complete
anatomy of *Rabutinage*, Bussy's secret history, reflects features of
Voiture's style and a strikingly complete arsenal of Voltairean
satirical devices. Special combinations of restraint, tact, and under-
statement vie in it with their opposites, freedom, bluntness, hyperbole. Textures of conventional language are cut by discordant
words from other codes, the languages of war or commerce (both
in the case of Mme d'Olonne) among others, that make satiric
intention maliciously clear. A low word may be called for, understood, then replaced by elegant periphrasis, or periphrasis by unexpected bluntness.[9]

Disgruntled by Bussy's satirical portrait, Mme de Sévigné still
conceded it to be fiendishly well written (7.26.68) and with good
reason. It reflects, as does the whole book, conversation she
enjoyed with Bussy and in her letters in unbuttoned and uncensored
moments. He describes it vividly in the portrait: "If one has wit,
especially playful wit, one has only to seek her company. She
understands, enters in, second-guesses, takes you further than you
meant to go. Sometimes she opens new territory, the heat of the
joke carries her away and she joyously accepts any freedom you
wish to be understood, provided it be veiled. She sometimes responds with compound interest, deeming that she would not acquit
herself if she did not go you one better." This is the "springtime of
humor" and "sprightly expression" that charmed, but also closed

the Prince d'Harcourt's door. Its freedom stops just short of the explicit ribaldry Bussy enjoyed with the Prince de Conti, in burlesques of techniques of fashionable novels,[10] and it starts anew whenever the cousins come together. "Hurry home," she bids him (3.14.49), "so that we may enjoy, both of us, ridiculing everything that deserves ridiculing." With Bussy such was the full joy of *Rabutinage*.

An early letter shows this prolonged pleasure of conversation. With a mixture of directness verging on insult and ironic play on the languages of heraldry, combat, compliment, it is an apprentice's appreciative imitation:

You are a pretty fellow not to have written to me for two months. Have you forgotten who I am and the rank I hold in the family? I will make you remember, little *cadet*, and if you anger me I will reduce you to a lower implantation in our arms. You knew that I was at the end of a pregnancy, and I find no more concern from you than if I were still a girl. Well, I have to inform you, and you may become as furious as you please, that I have given birth to a boy, who will suckle hatred of you with his milk, and that I intend to have a great many more for the sole purpose of making you enemies. You have not had the wit to do as much, fine begetter of girls. But I cannot conceal my affection. . . . I do violence to my feelings. . . . M. de Sévigné and I both love you very much and often talk of the pleasures of having you with us. (3.15.48)

The response was a lesson from the master. "I must tell you, Madame, that you take on a certain tone of chiding me that is more that of a mistress than a friend. Take care . . . once I am resolved to suffer, I shall wish the indulgences as well as the punishments of a lover. . . . You abuse my submission. It is true that you are as prompt in subsiding as in anger."

It did not take Mme de Sévigné long to learn that for Bussy a certain performance had always to be accomplished in letters that could not be given quite the tone she took with Ménage or anyone else. As early as 1654 Bussy too was ready to change tone, to undiluted if stylized praise. "Good Lord, my cousin: what wit you possess! How well you write! How adorable you are! Sometimes I condemn your insensitivity, sometimes I excuse it, but I always admire you. What, my cousin! Say sweet things to me and then forbid me the greatest affection for you. Very well, one must wish what you wish and love you after your own fashion" (7.30.54). The last concession is prophetic, a gesture that will be repeated as the only means of calming or maintaining at all the tempestuous correspondence.

Mme de Sévigné shares Bussy's evident pleasures in letter-writing. She tends with him to self-consciousness, curbing verbal inventiveness of her own[11] and imitating ornaments of his style (riddle, mixture of prose and verse, among others). She imitates beyond all else his irony, its half-serious play with fictions and the special twists that brevity and directness give to spying out ridicule. Conscious that this is only a part of her own style, she admits it: "Each person has his own style; mine, as you see, is not laconic" (7.19.55). So will she to Pomponne. As in 1681 Bussy is quite ready to recognize excellence in difference, given his motto, and responds with a "Be yourself" that Mme de Sévigné had long been used to hearing and wished to hear again: "For all of not being laconic, your style does not fail to be agreeable. I would be vexed if it were shorter" (8.13.55).

Time and trouble brought new combats and trials and different lessons. In 1658 a squabble over money, felt as a breach of friendship on both sides, interrupted friendly relations. The satirical portrait, a "sin of the writer," brought a rupture that took almost a decade to heal. Mme de Sévigné neither congratulated Bussy on his election to the Academy in 1665 nor consoled him with a visit during the imprisonment that ended the same year for him in the Bastille. When the epistolary dialogue is renewed, ostensibly for Bussy's consolation in exile, it is fitful and difficult for at least five years and never really the pleasure it once had been.

A model "litigation letter" (7.26.68) shows the altered tone of the new "combat." Blood tie and family wit are set aside, supposedly in an eminently Bussy-like concern for setting the record straight, and with them go sympathy for exile and isolation. "I won't tell you the extreme interest I have always taken in your fortune. You would take it only as *rabutinage*. But it is not, it is you. It is you too who have caused me sad and bitter affliction when I saw three new Marshals of France. Mme de Villars, who received calls, put me in mind of those I would have had on such an occasion if you had wished." Real consolation? It was not felt so by Bussy, who heard vindictive payment in like terms for "bitter affliction" of a material and spiritual betrayal.

Admitting the portrait "a ridiculous piece," confessing earlier "guilt," Bussy in full submission offers "a thousand pardons." Without banter that might be misread, he answers the demands of the twenty-sixth, "consulting his heart," as he clearly implies she might do. "You should be consoled once for all. . . . I, who am the interested party and neither insensate nor silly, see with the scorn of a persecuted man of honor. . . . When I see caprices of fortune as ridiculous as this, far from being distressed I rejoice that such a promotion is an honor to my disgrace. . . . And those are the feelings that my friends should have for me" (8.29.68). The "pupil" is no longer willing to accept this lesson on form. Smarting from her own sense of persecuted honor, she will not yet adapt her style to Bussy's new self-image of "persecuted man of honor," as she later does in the letters Bussy felt her finest to him.

Bussy's letter went unanswered. Preparations for her daughter's wedding and troublesome inquiry about the family's titles of nobility preoccupied Mme de Sévigné. After seeking information on them, a "matter of the honor of our house" (8.14.68), she set about the difficult response, with confessed weariness and irritated quotation of his phrase from the portrait. "Nothing is lost on me," that "dog of a portrait, done and done up."

The joy of having done it so well, and being applauded, caused you to find all the wrongs in the world on my side and thereby to rid yourself of guilt. Mme de Montglas obliged you to tear it up and then her husband put it all back together again! What silliness! . . . If he did return it, you had only to put it into your strongbox and not let it circulate and fall into the hands of Mme de La Baume and be translated into every language. . . .[12] It is purely your fault. . . . As for my not seeming angry when I first saw it, make no mistake about it, M. le Comte, I was furious. I spent whole nights without sleep. . . . When I saw myself given up to the public and circulated in all the provinces I confess that I was in despair, and when I did not see you— which would have restored me and my old affection for you, I gave in to that dryness of heart that did not permit me to do anything else during your imprisonment than what I did. . . . Without pushing this further, for the last time I give you for penance, for punishment, meditation on the full affection I have always had for you, on my innocence in the first alleged offense, on all my confidence in our reconciliation. . . . *Basta*, here endeth the trial. (8.28)

As an apparent mark of renewed confidence, Mme de Sévigné closes with worries about her children. For the moment, significantly, they are equally divided, between worry over Françoise-

Marguerite's remaining unmarried and Charles's departure at sea
for the siege of Candia. He had been encouraged by Turenne, Retz,
La Rochefoucauld. "They all approved so strongly that the thing
was decided before I knew anything. He left. I wept bitterly. I will
not have a moment of rest during his entire voyage. I see all the
perils and am dead from seeing them." In this letter where petu-
lance and anger set a good deal slightly askew, this last outburst
catches perhaps more than a hint of the ridicule of Molière's miser
Harpagon, "dying, dead, buried" when he imagines the theft of his
treasure.

Sensing real hurt behind these Rabutin theatrics, of the mother
who had not been consulted, real weariness and bid for sympathy,
Bussy found the right tone in response, his old tone, heightened
with precious hyperboles (8.31.68). "You moved me furiously, and
I will tell you in two words that I love and esteem no one more than
you." Shifting back to the metaphor of combat he closes (after
conjuring up an appropriate shepherdess to cap off his consolation)
in the familiar tone of ritual gallantry. "What will one not do or
must one not do to regain a heart as upright as that I've lost? . . .
One could not be less capable of a third charge than I, lovely
cousin; why would you oblige me to it? I have surrendered arms in
the reply I made. I asked for my life; you wished to kill me on the
ground, and that is a little inhuman. . . . If you are not yet content
with my terms, send me a model of the satisfaction you wish, and I
will send it back countersigned by a secretary and sealed with my
arms. What more can be necessary?" No more seemed to be.
"Rise, Comte, I have no wish to kill you on the ground or to take
your sword to begin combat anew," his cousin answered to this
gallant submission (9.4.68).

But begin anew they both did, and Corbinelli,[13] the lively Italian
scholar who participated in their pleasures of writing after 1658,
sent up a prayer of intercession: "You are two true Rabutins, made
for one another. God keep you in perfect intelligence" (6.17.70).
Sense and sense of humor again both disappeared as Bussy took
offense over Grignan's failure to write him, as was fitting, before
marrying Françoise-Marguerite. Relieved by the marriage and
happy to have her daughter yet with her in Paris, Mme de Sévigné
chose to continue the old vein. She made light of the offense,
thereby gave new offense, and finally retreated to new recitals of
Bussy's past errors (8.8.69; 6.17.70).

First "passage at arms" in this third break in friendship (6.4.69) at the moment of her daughter's marriage could not contrast more vividly with the letter by the appreciative imitator written when Charles was born. Like the letter of August 28, 1668, whose anger made Bussy bow to punishment, it is a declaration of independence. In what Bussy found "affected raillery" she displays unmistakable mastery of his style that amounts to pastiche, criticizes, finally condescends by asking for a "Bussy-letter" for her son-in-law. "Your letters always please me," she begins, then delivers the blows: "Don't for that reason begin to 'love me hopelessly,' as you threaten to do. What would you have me do with your 'hopelessly' at the point of becoming a grandmother. . . . You are an excessive man. Is it not odd that you cannot find something between offending me outrageously and loving me more than life?" Again using the portrait, which had pinpointed her chameleon nature, she exults sarcastically in a new state of peace and well-being that Bussy might reflect and share, if *he* now "consulted *his* heart"; "I am so constant, so at peace and in repose that your bubblings do not profit you as they might elsewhere." The final request is a calculated insult; Grignan, she assures, "until now has esteemed and liked you. I pray you, Comte, write him a bantering letter, the kind you know so well how to write. You will give me pleasure, I who love you, and also him, just between us, the most desirable husband and the most divine for society." Bussy has a rival.

Faced with Bussy's displeasure, Mme de Sévigné persists and offers a last blow that preludes another gap in correspondence. "I wanted to banter a bit with you, and you were a hundred leagues from it. Is it you, Comte, who did not like my last letter? Is it you who answered it? Don't hope that I shall not keep yours and hope someday you will return to the good sense that was so agreeable. . . . Not only do I not recognize my blood in your style. I don't recognize yours. If that were to continue, we could be bled all we pleased without fearing to weaken each other" (6.9.69). Corbinelli might well intervene; someone needed to do so.

From correspondence with Bussy, which closes Mme de Sévigné's apprenticeship, the letter-writer learns much. If at first she sharpens her wit on his, by 1670 she has sharpened her mind by dealing with real misunderstandings, strains, breaks in communication. Allowed no pirouettes under Bussy's knowing eye, she is forced to face *real* confrontation and becomes conscious of the implications of letter-writing as confrontation.

Misunderstanding is a function of distance and time. Clear and direct explanations of feeling and expressions of it that will stand scrutiny are emotion's demands for overcoming distance. As the effort to "set things straight" proceeds, a time lag intervenes. Distance obscures changes in the lives of the correspondents. Changes felt essential to one writer are scarcely perceived or are unrecognized by the other, who sees from and speaks to a past image no longer vital. Confronted with inevitable time warp and compulsions to "say it all," the successful "performance" of letter-writing brings with its very success a falsification and "betrayal," a trick image whose resemblance to self-image the writer is loath but then forced to admit. "Dryness of heart" it is for the woman who celebrates a "heart like mine" and a "style filled with affection," out of phase with a new Bussy's inner time of exile, first inadvertently then with purposeful scorn. Shallow and hollow mannerism it becomes for a man who prides himself on "naturalness in all things" and style that is its mirror, out of phase with a new Sévigné's affective life after her daughter's marriage, awkwardly then with intentional sarcasm.

Letter-writing and epistolary style, Mme de Sévigné understands from exchanges with Bussy, always lag in the past. They are always behind in reflecting fully appropriate recognition of a present lived in the moment. When one correspondent receives an "answer," he is already "someone else." Epistolary style must be ever changing along with life's changes. But as they are missed, it takes on a life of its own, a life of performance. The life in the reading escapes destructively from the orderly symbolic life given to the letter in its writing. If both correspondents admit that they bring out the best in each other when together, and could say everything in conversation, both are forced to recognize that quite the opposite is possible when separated and forced to live through their letters. For Mme de Sévigné while writing to her daughter this experience will always be a "dragon," a lingering fear of failure, but also a constant challenge to the mind.

III   *Grignan*

For Mlle de Sévigné a "prince charming" was a puzzlingly long time in coming, her mother mused. "The name 'the prettiest maiden in France' is a most agreeable one," she wrote to Bussy, "but I am weary of doing the honors for her" (7.26.68). Stunningly beautiful and graceful at Court, where she shone more often than had been possible for her mother at a less brilliant moment in its history, yet without really serious suitors, "her fate is so difficult to understand that I am at a loss" (8.28.68). Mother and daughter of course set sights very high, though not so high as Mlle de Sévigné's beauty perhaps reached, when we hear it complimented in the fable La Fontaine dedicated to her—"The Lion in Love" (IV.1). "Love is a strange master/Happy he who knows it/Only in a story. . . ."

During festivities at Versailles on July 18, after the production of Molière's *George Dandin* (that burlesque of ridiculous misalliance), Mme de Sévigné found her twenty-two-year-old daughter and herself at the King's table. She heard gossip that her daughter might go even farther. Bussy heard it, too, and was delighted to speculate on having a royal mistress in the family (Lalanne ed., 7.17.68). Broadsides unfortunately hinted that Louis might not be the first.[14] Another mother might have ignored them and been as delighted as Bussy. Feeling as she did about the King and no doubt clearsighted about the ultimate fate of royal mistresses, Mme de Sévigné like the father in La Fontaine's fable took her precautions, with speed and energy, to keep her "princess" from harm's way.

François Adhémar de Monteil, Comte de Grignan, was by no means a "prince charming." "Not the most handsome lad but one of the greatest gentlemen of the realm," Mme de Sévigné wrote to Bussy. He would obviously more than do, for the mother, who praises his assets in a cynically practical tone and with bravado calculated to make Bussy forget that "approval" is sought two months after the fact and to persuade him as she had herself. "All his wives have died to give place to your cousin, and even his father and son, by an extraordinary goodness. So being richer than he has ever been, and by birth, establishment, and good qualities all we might wish, we are not making him any of the usual difficulties and trust the two families that preceded us. He seems quite pleased with the alliance, and as soon as we have news from his uncle the Archbishop of Arles (his other uncle the Bishop of Uzès is here), the affair will be concluded before the end of the year. . . . People seem content, and that is a great deal; one is stupid enough almost to go by that" (12.4.68). Determination and speed, for the reason lightly veiled in closing, are the order of the day; scruples in qualifying this good fortune are not.

The Grignans could satisfy any proud Rabutin. They were one of the oldest aristocratic families of Provence, which remained important and respected in church and magistracy. The fact that Grignan was twice widowed, with two daughters, may be as easily glossed over as discrepancy in age (at thirty-six, nearer the mother's). But in the matter of finances there is a purposeful misrepresentation. Income, estimated at 500,000 francs, looks princely enough, until it is known, as Mme de Sévigné did, that debts encumbered three quarters of it.[15] Given this, lawsuits in the offing, and the ruinous expenses of maintaining the vast Château of Grignan, the mother's confidence is plainly wishful thinking. The responsibilities she assumed in payment for it weighed heavily in her future.

To provide Mlle de Sévigné with a fitting and seductive dowry (equal to Grignan's debts) her mother borrowed heavily. The purchase, also in 1669, of a first commission for Charles, still having full share in her concerns, forced arrangements that must have made the good Abbé de Coulanges shake a head that had already paused over Grignan's situation. But the Marquise pushed on. Loan payments amounting to half her income proved immediately difficult, forced sale of land (La Baudrière, "from which only grain comes," she remarked with cheerful abandon), and were not completed until 1689. Symbolically, as in fact, interest on the debt of 1669 remained to be paid throughout her life.[16]

Two facts about Grignan in the mother's mind carried the day. First, he and therefore his wife could reside in Paris. Not alone in his charge as Lieutenant-General for Languedoc, he did not need to reside there. He was also a man of the world, known from earlier acquaintance at the Rambouillets. Fine taste in writing, the ways of society, especially music, wit (that took jokes on lack of good looks in good part) were remembered. Very soon after the wedding on January 29, 1669, Mme de Sévigné leased a large house in the rue de Thorigny (behind the present No. 8) where the enlarged family could enjoy life as the large Coulanges family had. It may have seemed to her that honors missed by not being cousin of a Marshal of France would be more than compensated by a salon there in which the joys and elegance of Mme de Rambouillet's might be reborn. Grignan eased anxieties. Neither an enemy nor, perhaps she thought, a real rival for her daughter's love, he would be a son-in-law with whom she would be able to live and talk with ease and to confide in, in her own way, about her daughter. In short, with Grignan she could remain herself, triumph over present threats to happiness, recapture that of the past and ensure its future. Grignan and Bussy might not get on especially well, but they spoke the same language, and Mme de Sévigné writes to her son-in-law much as she did to Bussy on good days.

Pregnant with Mme de Sévigné's first grandchild, Marie-Blanche, Mme de Grignan remained in Paris, to her mother's relief and delight, for eight months after her husband's departure for a new appointment in Provence that had undone the well-laid plans. The series of eight letters Mme de Sévigné wrote to him, from August through December 1670, are remarkable. Cheerfully newsy and recreative, "bagatelles" requiring no responses, she professed, they could not be more serious in some matters and called anxiously for answers that to her relief—and through her art—came as she wished to crown her epistolary successes.

Intimacy deftly sets a tone of concern for the Grignans and their affairs that might otherwise sound shocking. "Let us speak no more of that woman," she writes with play on the rivalries of the old banter, and admits for the first time under shelter of that tone: "We love her beyond all reason. . . . Mme de Coulanges writes me that you love me; although that is not news, I am pleased that your affection has resisted absence and Provence and is sometimes felt" (11.28.70). But what is truly remarkable here and in all the letters to Grignan is less this banter than the direct and indirect use made of it to reduce, with the apparent artlessness and ease of conversation, tensions of the newly separated family that the letters reflect.

Grignan would not press his mother-in-law on her qualifications for writing: "I am very discerning on the matter of affection and know it not too badly. I confess to you that I am content with that which I see and which is all that I might wish" (8.15.70). He could only be edified by the image of the two women reading Nicole's *Moral Essays* together. "Nothing comes from him but perfection," she judges in the first allusion to reading that had a special place in later years, all the more special for having begun in common with her daughter. The expert testimony comes from a "character witness" who in more than one letter covertly labors to set

Grignan's mind at rest on any possibility of gossip about his wife.

Haven't I truly given you the prettiest wife in the world? Can one be more
upright, more as she should be? Can one love you more tenderly? Can one
have more Christian attitudes? Can one wish more passionately to be with
you? And can one be more attached to all duties? It is quite ridiculous for
me to say so many good things about my daughter, but I admire her as
others do, the more so for being near her, the more too for seeing her more
scrupulous in little things than I would have thought, assured though I was
of her observation of the important ones. I assure you that people give her
her due and that she doesn't want for the praises she merits. . . . She complains every day about being kept here and says very seriously that it is
cruel to have separated her from you. . . . I pray you to calm her mind. . . .
Nothing was more impossible than taking her with you in her condition
and nothing better for her health, and reputation even, than her giving
birth here. (8.6.70)

If combat on Mme de Grignan's *gloire*, or over this style filled with
affection and admiration, was expected, none was engaged. But
another serious trial awaited.

In a note of moving brevity (11.19.70) Mme de Grignan apologized to her husband four days after Marie-Blanche's birth that it
was a daughter she had given him, expressed her desire to join him,
and handed the pen to her mother to fill in details. A lively account
of the event and a flurry of banter follow in which intercalated
news of a friend betrays the writer's worried distraction at a
moment when written expression of distress seems inadequate.
"What more shall I say? Dare I write more? I believe that the
health of your wife will console you, while our dear Duchesse de
Saint-Simon has smallpox so dangerously that her life is feared.
Adieu, my dear, I leave your poor heart to sort out all these
feelings. You have long known mine for you."

Grignan's response is a deliverance. Significantly, roles have
been exchanged. Assurance now comes from him. Much needed at
the moment it repays all the mother's earlier letter-writing and confirms her opinion that her son-in-law is all that she thought. "Mme
de Coulanges has written me more than four times that you love me
with all your heart, that you speak of me and wish for me. As I
have made all the advances in this affection and loved you first,
you can judge how content my heart is to learn that you respond to
the inclination I have so long felt for you. All that you write about

your daughter is admirable. I had no doubt that the good health of my daughter would console you for everything. . . . I must truly love you to send her to you in such a bad season. What folly it is to leave such a good mother, *with whom you assure me she is content*, to go off in search of a man at the other end of France" (12.10.70, my emphasis).

Nothing in Mme de Sévigné's correspondence contradicts Grignan's assertion after her death that his mother-in-law had always been a friend, valued for her concern and advice, with whom he found pleasure. The achievement of her first letters to him is their final contribution to the understanding that made that relationship possible. Continuing tensions existed, but neither between them nor husband and wife. Mother and daughter lived out the tensions.

Mme de Grignan's daily complaints about separation and her passionate will to be with her husband are not fictions invented by her mother for him. Françoise-Marguerite at first must have been relieved to have her mother's talent undertake touchy matters of reassurance. But a real rivalry came to be felt that is not concealed by Mme de Sévigné's light tone in dealing with it. "She is in despair that you have written to me. I have never seen a woman so jealous and envious. Well, it's to no avail. I defy her to prevent our friendship." She quickly gave up this tone, taking pains to avoid feelings of the reality of that kind of tension. Tactfully she concludes her letter: "I forbid you to write to me, but not to love me" (9.12.70).

Grignan's reassurance that his wife is content with her mother is especially welcome at the moment of Mme de Grignan's departure. The last letter to him before it reveals a tension that all the old style cannot finally lessen. Convinced as she may have been earlier of her daughter's passionate determination to join her husband, the force of its reality nonetheless surprises her. She bows to it, as Bussy does to the ways of love, to a drama she is forced to play by the "folly" of separation and love "beyond all reason." She candidly admits that separation may be relief. "I want to tell you that I don't feel the pleasure of having her at the moment. I know that she must leave. Neither her duty nor her affairs keep her here. We have only a heavy heart and talk incessantly of roads and rains and tragic stories of travelers. In a word, although I love her, as you know I do, the state we are in at the moment depresses and pains us. In these last days there has been no delight."

Against real odds Mme de Sévigné's faith in her son-in-law was repaid. Even with worries over financial difficulties, litigation, political intrigue in Provence, the Grignans' marriage was on the whole a good one. Grignan was as devoted to his family as to his administrative responsibilities. That devotion brought a special embarrassment of riches also not calculated by the prospective mother-in-law until she was forced to do so.

To her remark that "all Grignan's wives have died," Bussy replied nastily that Grignan had worn them out (satirists nicknamed him "Tomcat"). "The only thing that makes me fear for the prettiest maiden in France is that Grignan, not yet old, is already on his third wife: he goes through them like suits of clothes or at least carriages" (12.8.68). Yearly pregnancies were Mme de Grignan's lot, the bane of aristocratic wives, whose families in a period of high infant mortality depended for influence and wealth on male progeny. If special pains were taken to "console" Grignan after Marie-Blanche's birth, they were the more necessary since it was a second "failure" of Mme de Grignan, who had suffered miscarriage the previous year, and there was as yet no male heir. Mme de Sévigné was compelled to follow seven pregnancies, six in six years, two miscarriages, and the birth of a deformed child, a melancholy history reconstructed for us by Gérard-Gailly.[17] She saw the progressive degeneration of the children, from congenital bone malformation, it seems, and accompanying deterioration of her daughter's health. Bussy's words may have come to mind and with them a "reproach" on her choice of son-in-law. If they did, it was in silence, well covered by an incessantly busy flow of recommendations of restorative remedies, diet, rest, and also in advance of her time, of birth control.

With the departure of Mme de Grignan for Provence, time is told by Mme de Sévigné according to several calendars. The schedule of loan and interest payments exacted its attention. It was less exigent than the rigorously followed menstrual cycles of her daughter. Most of all she came to live according to the time-tables of the postal service that gave structure to her life, a service reformed by Louvois but which remained a careless servant when it seemed one's life depended on it.

CHAPTER 4

Absence (1671-1673)

DURING the eighteen months of first separation from her daughter, letter-writing takes a new place in Mme de Sévigné's life. Twice weekly she sealed her packet of letters, dispatched with regularity that rivals the efficiency of the post itself. The 138 "dispatches" contain more letters than are extant for Mme de Sévigné's first forty-five years. Bussy by striking contrast had to be content with six letters. After rather perfunctory renewal of epistolary relations (2.16.71), he complains of neglect (5.24.71), then resigns himself testily to it (1.28.72), suspecting rightly that the better part of Mme de Sévigné's time and the best of her mind are concentrated on her daughter.

I *First Separation*

The most dramatized moment in all Mme de Sévigné's correspondence is the departure of her daughter's carriage, on February 4, 1671, from the house in the rue de Thorigny. The receding carriage, like her daughter's empty room, became an obsessive image of loss, which haunted her long after first reunion in July 1672.

Two days before departure Mme de Grignan had been made the special gift of a newly set diamond ring. As with the marriage vow, it symbolized enduring love, a first pledge of "unequaled tenderness," which shines in the formulas of tenderness of the mother's first letters and outshines mere maternal love. "May it remind you of me and the inordinate tenderness I have for you and, no matter what, of how many ways I would like always to show it" (2.2.71). A letter written during a difficult moment from Livry (recently redated 6.1.69) made a similar pledge. Resetting emotion as the diamond will be, the unchanging presence in thought of the absent

loved one is presented as a keepsake, appropriately "mounted" in
a "fine letter."

I am writing this letter in the garden, as you imagined it. The nightingales
and little birds have received your greeting with great pleasure but without
great respect. Their setting divests them of humility. Yesterday I spent two
hours alone with the hamadryads. I spoke of you, and their response gave
me great contentment. I don't know whether the countryside is content
with me, for finally after enjoying all its beauties I can only say, "Whatever you have, you do not have Calliste/And I find nothing when I do not
see her.". . .[1]

For memory's sake, a moment of dignity would be the perfect
gift for Mme de Grignan's leave-taking. But Mme de Sévigné first
threw herself at the horses, then rushed away to an upper window,
there feeling and doubtless showing the temptation to end her life
she later recalled (3.3.71). Leave-taking could scarcely have been
more difficult for the daughter, who must inevitably have felt some
relief to have it behind her. For the mother, fear of that relief
became another obsession. Another obstacle to future reunion?
But her first concern, subsuming all else, was how to express fully
the emotion that separation and loss had brought with new intensity into her life.
Bereavement beyond language is evoked by fragmentation in the
first troubled letter. Loss seems to have destroyed the past, as the
death of a loved one does, to close possibilities of reunion as surely
as do last rites. Absence in this nightmare is the only reality; earlier
separations and letters during them seem counterfeits of experience.

My affliction would be mediocre indeed if I could describe it, so I shall not
try. I search everywhere for my dear child, I do not find her, and her every
step takes her farther from me. In this state I went to Sainte-Marie, always
weeping and always dying. It seemed my heart and soul had been torn from
my body. How cruel separation is! I asked to be alone and was led to Mme
du Housset's room and given a fire. Agnès stayed with me, without
speaking, as agreed. I spent five hours sobbing. Every thought brought
death. I wrote to M. de Grignan, in a tone you can imagine. I went to see
Mme de Lafayette, who renewed my sorrow by her sympathy. She was
alone, ill, afflicted by the death of a friend, in the right state for me. M. de
La Rochefoucauld came. They spoke of you, of how right I was to be
concerned. . . . About eight I came home, and entering, good Lord, do you

know how I felt going up the stairs? That room I always entered was open, but empty and in disorder. Your poor little girl there made me see mine. Do you really know how I suffered? After awakening more than once to darkness, the morning came without my having advanced one step toward peace of mind. The afternoon was spent with Mme de La Troche at the Arsenal. In the evening I received your letter, which brought back the violence of my first emotions, and I shall finish mine this evening at the Coulanges with some news. You know all my news when you know the afflictions of everyone you left here. . . . (2.6.71)

Every desperate movement and painful hour brings the shattering fact of loss, expressed as a death of the spirit. Like the poet of Hugo's "Tomorrow at Dawn," Mme de Sévigné has set out on a single-minded pilgrimage after memories that blocks out all else. The convent in the Faubourg Saint-Jacques where her daughter had briefly boarded, not the family chapel nearby, is the first pilgrimage site. There peace is sought in a bare room, not in the Mass, under eyes that respect her own ritual. Suffused with her daughter's image, the mother's spirit is no more refreshed by this "retreat" than by the night's fitful sleep. In the meanwhile, epistolary initiative, through weakness as much as tact, was left to the daughter, quick to begin it when scarcely outside Paris.

The chronicles of letters that stretch the first days into weeks evoke a life propelled by unrelenting movement as eloquently as do Pascal's thoughts on "diversion," perturbation of mind alienated from God, which had appeared the month before Mme de Grignan's departure. Time, a wealth of leisure once spent with abandon, weighs heavily. The former delight of society offers no joy and is shunned. First visits to close friends and relatives seem scarcely to have taken place (2.9.71). Her granddaughter's presence only accentuates the feeling of her own daughter's absence. In morning installments of responses to them, Mme de Grignan's letters offer joy and consolation, but by evening both are as elusive as the compensations of society and other friendships. Then letter-writing only revives the reality of absence and intensifies the silence of rooms empty of direct exchanges of shared affection. In the mother's distorted perceptions, the gesture of the smile is severed from its symbolic equivalence in letters; letters take on the gravity of an enigma and seem the vehicle of some menacing irony or mystery.[2]

I have received your letters, *ma bonne*,[3] as you have my ring. I dissolve in tears reading them, and it seems as though my heart wants to break in half. It seems as though you were writing insults to me, as though you were ill or had suffered some accident, and the opposite is true. You love me, my dear child, and tell me so in a way I cannot bear without many tears; you continue your voyage without mishap, and when I know that I know what gives me greatest pleasure. Such is my state. You divert yourself by thinking of me, speaking of me, and like to write better than to give voice to your feelings. However they come, they are received with tenderness and feeling that can be understood only by those who love as I do. You make me feel all tenderness is capable of feeling. But if you think of me, my poor *bonne*, be assured that I think of you continually. It is what the devout call habitual thought and what we ought to have for God, were we to do our duty. Nothing distracts me from it. I am always with you. I see that carriage continuing its journey, taking you ever farther. . . . I have only two of your letters, perhaps a third will come. That is the only consolation I wish and seek no others. I am entirely incapable of being in a crowd. The Duchesses de Verneuil and d'Arpajon have tried, but I have excused myself. I have never seen such beautiful souls as I have found here. I spent all Saturday talking about you and crying with Mme de Villars, who shared my feelings deeply. Yesterday I went to hear the Bishop of Agen preach, to see Mme du Puisieux, the Bishop of Uzès, and Mme du Puy-du-Fou. . . . Today I shall take supper with Mme de Lafayette. Those are my carnival festivities. I have a Mass said for you every day—that devotion is not chimerical. (2.9.71)

The closing of February 9 is far from a conventional formula, as it sets the final terms of real consolation: "Adieu, my dear child, unique passion of my life, the pleasure and pain of my life. Love me always. That is the only thing that can give me consolation." It reflects "in beauty" acceptance of a new life of feeling, found in solitude greater than any known before, a new sense of ambivalence pervading experience after first separation and thereafter always beneath the surface of letters. Now "life is cruelly mixed with bitterness" (*absinthe*, 2.17.72), its savor as though tinged abrasively by the medicinal herb. Letter-writing, experience reaffirms, will always be a mixed pleasure, a second-best reality. With its own "grandeur and wretchedness," as Pascal understood those warring contraries that shatter moments of balance, letter-writing exalts by its illusion of consoling presence, then plunges the writer to the depths at the moment of withdrawal from its elusive symbolic reunion.

With balance, gained in new reflectiveness, the closing "in beauty" begins an extraordinary collection of professions of love, rephrased with "artistic" searching for fresh expression more deliberate and obvious in closings than at any other moment of letter-writing. Sometimes they recall the salons (or memoirs, like Mme de Motteville's caressing of the life of Anne of Austria); often they suggest an artist's appreciation of the form bringing reality to his vision. "You know how I love your beauty," the mother recalls (2.27.71) as she brings it to life. But these means to an end reenact most often moments of a mother's pleasure and pride in closeness and touching when they most matter in the lives of mother and daughter. Just as she rediscovers those pleasures watching her granddaughter "embellish each day," she regains them at the moment of parting in her letters—"You kiss and embrace me tenderly: . . . I kiss your beautiful cheeks and beautiful breast with all my heart" (4.8.71). Closings like this perpetually replay and master the moment of first leavetaking, transforming it by graceful and reflective gestures into the adieu that had then been physically impossible.

Forced emotionally to the impossible demand "show me your love always," the letter-writer accepts its risks and transposes her consciousness of its nature—"inordinate," "beyond reason," into the register of a spiritual drama worthy of Corneille and the lucidity of his Cinna that seemed to her sublime. "I am mad for Corneille," she wrote, quoting the playwright's self-description as "the hand that composed the soul of great Pompey and the mind of Cinna" (3.9.72), but substitutes her own word "love" for Corneille's "mind." Her renewed pledge is Cinna's, in the passionate soliloquy at the center of Corneille's play. "My faith, my heart, my hand, all is pledged to you./All that I do evermore is by your leave" (vv. 895-96). The pledge is made during the first Holy Week of the "new life" from the garden of her uncle's abbey at Livry. Seeking peace where it had been found before, and release from exhausting tensions of Paris in spiritual retreat, the letter-writer prepared herself by composing the regular letter to her daughter in advance. What she found in the solitude of Livry was a repetition of the experience of her first letter, which amplifies already humbling awareness of weakness and limitation. Consciousness of spiritual failure, to transcend the bondage of love, is expressed in letters unmatched in power by those of any other woman of her time.[4]

I propose to be in solitude. I shall make a little Trappist monastery. I want to pray and reflect. I am resolved to fast strictly, to walk to make up for all the time I have kept to my room, above all to humble myself for the love of God. But what I shall observe better than all that, my poor *bonne*, is to think of you. I have not stopped since I arrived, and as I am no longer capable of containing my feelings I have begun to write to you at the end of the little shady walk you are fond of, on a bank of moss where I have seen you lying. But, good Lord, what place is there where I have not seen you? How all those thoughts crowd in upon my heart! There is not a place in the house, the church, the countryside, the garden, where I have not seen you and which does not bestow a memory that wounds my heart. I think and think again of it all. . . . My dear child I love so passionately is two hundred leagues from me, no longer with me. I cannot keep from crying, I am exhausted, my dear *bonne*. This is a great weakness, but I cannot find strength against tenderness so just and natural. . . . I pray you not to speak of my weakness, but love it yourself and respect tears that come from a heart wholly yours. (3.24.71)

Alone like Cinna, feeling his conflicting shame and exaltation, Mme de Sévigné accepts the renewed pledge of love with full lucidity that must be heard. In this privileged moment at Livry, with a fullness of life bestowed by involuntary memory and prolonged in writing, she chooses to seek her own salvation in the past of memory and to make of it the living heart of her letters, which chart and contain both her present and future.

Had I shed as many tears for my sins as I have for you since arriving here, I should be in excellent disposition to observe my Easter. . . . I passed the time here as I proposed except for memories of you, which tormented me more than I had anticipated. How strange a powerful imagination is! It represents things as though still existing, one is present as in a dream, and with a heart like mine that is to die. I do not know where to escape from you. The house in Paris renews my grief daily and Livry overwhelms me. Provence does not set me before your eyes as every place here does you to mine. I have found some sweetness in the sadness I have felt here. The deep solitude, the great silence, the sad office of the day, the devout singing of *tenebrae* (I have never before been at Livry during Holy Week), the fasting, and the beauty of the garden that would charm you have all given me pleasure. Alas, how I have wished you here! . . . But I must return to Paris tomorrow. I shall find your letters and go hear Bourdaloue or Mascaron preach the Passion—I have always venerated fine passions. Adieu, my dear Countess, you will hear no more of me from Livry. I'll finish my letter in

Paris. If I had had the strength not to write to you from here and to make a sacrifice to God of all I have felt, it would have been worth more than all the penances in the world. But instead of making good use of the retreat I have sought consolation only in writing to you about it. Ah, my *bonne*, how weak and wretched. . . . (3.26.71)

Is, was, and ever will be, Mme de Grignan must be convinced. A well-known sermonette from the austere Arnauld d'Andilly, father of the Arnauld clan, on the danger of making an idol in her heart "as dangerous as any other though it may seem less criminal" (4.29.71), does not divert the letter-writer from ritual observance of the "new cult." It too is capable of liturgical rhythms—"Finally everything turns on you, or from you, or for you, or by you" (3.24.71).[5] Special observances are made, with delicately turned reminiscence that did not leave Mme de Grignan untouched, in "Bourdalouing," for example, excursions to hear the eloquence Mme de Sévigné preferred to all other from the pulpit. Affected by Bourdaloue's vivid pictures of contemporary life (like the Maréchal de Gramont, who amused her [4.13.72] by breaking a solemn moment with "Merciful heavens, he's right!"), she was moved also by his preaching on death. But even listening to him, the spell of real eloquence comes from elsewhere. "Everyone was at the sermon, and it was worthy of its audience. I thought of you twenty times and as many wished you at my side. You would have been delighted to hear it, and I to watch you listening to it" (3.13.71).

Ambivalence and paradox are a part of the letter-writer's new life from which she cannot by her own means escape. Love wills it thus, as Bussy might have said and the mother repeats countless times after the paradox of the impossible, nonrational demand "show me your love always," examined on February 9. "You have no need of my sadness," "conserve the essence of your feelings but spare yourself tears," she wrote time after time, as she did on February 18. Recoiling from cruelty first felt in separation, then from awareness of inflicting it, the letter-writer is fully caught in this ambivalence, which the mother too often rediscovers in her avid quests after life-giving information. "You will hear no more of me from Livry," the letter-writer promises; "one must pass lightly over certain thoughts," she repeats echoing her daughter's counsel. But twice more Mme de Grignan is made to hear of sacraments interrupted by "habitual thought," again if more

calmly felt as spiritual backsliding (12.4.73; 6.5.75). And at Les
Rochers, where life is led with no Trappist aspirations, the pledge
of Livry is reechoed and followed to its final conclusion. Passionate
personal logic is expressed with directness expurgated by the first
editor (Perrin), who broke the link of Mme de Sévigné's bold
thought and resigned but still regretful confession of spiritual
tepidness. "Could treasures and all the goods of the earth give me
as much joy as your love?" she asks; then confronting sacrifice of
joys of another world, asks again: "Or could hell be worse than not
having it?" (8.9.71).

Like Origen (9.20.71), the mother would deny hell as eternal
punishment and find with his sanction a less dogmatic basis for a
personal religion, elaborated freely and without prejudice by the
mind. But it was epistolary dialogue and her daughter, not the
Church Father's *Ad Celsum*, that led the letter-writer's mind. The
paradox of love's unreason is a persistent pattern of letters per-
suading their reader of their message of inordinate tenderness. But
faced honestly and courageously, before Livry, the paradox is set
by the movement of the letter-writer's mind and shapes letters (e.g.,
2.9; 18.71). In introspective consciousness of limitations, Mme de
Sévigné's mind moves to a final term of paradox, which, in the
light of epistolary exchange, becomes fixed as self-definition of the
limit of her mind. "I believe as you do that there must be a little
grace and that philosophy alone cannot suffice. . . . I'm beginning
Nicole again. I would like to make a bouillon of it and swallow it"
(11.4.71).

With equal candor the letter-writer does not shrink from calling
to life in the letters of first separation a hell in which nudity and
madness (*folie*) are natural visions. Thinking back to the first day
she recalls "pain like illness" (6.7.71) and fears—"sometimes I am
mad" (3.3.71)—a reemerging blackness, when "it seems to me as
though I am completely naked, stripped of all that once made me
attractive" (2.11.71). To Bussy she wrote laconically of "black
vapors" (2.16.71).

The trauma of separation, "that thing apart in my life sus-
ceptible to no comparison" (5.18), naturally and on reflection
seemed like illness to the letter-writer. One contemporary clinician
might have been describing her, as Mme de Lafayette had, and as
she understood herself anew when separation suppressed habitual
functions, ruptured the fabric of life, and shattered her self-image.

"Women whose nature is little inclined to melancholy fall prey to it all the more seriously; 'they are cruelly used and violently disturbed by it, for melancholia being more opposed to their temperament, it removes them farther from their natural constitution.' "[6] In passionate emotion, with the cumulative emotional force of earlier losses that pushed her to express a child's dependent weakness and anxiety of abandonment, Mme de Sévigné saw what madness must *be like*, and like other contemporary moralists (La Rochefoucauld included) she links passion and madness. The "black inconstancy" and spiritual travail of baroque poems may seem at hand, as vapors, bile, and black chagrin reappear in the letters. The letter-writer likens herself to tear-shedding Niobe and gives herself to unreason as destructively as any character in Racine's *Andromaque* (quoted 3.11). "I will live to love you, and abandon my life to that love—to all its joy and all its pain, to all its pleasures and to all its anguish, to all the emotions that my passion can give me" (5.6). But that pledge is only half the story. "One is and is not one's own mistress" (2.17.72), she wrote with reflectiveness typically transcending momentary crisis (the last illness of her aunt Mme de La Trousse, who cannot be "sacrificed" for the journey to Provence) and the guide of a year-long battle for equilibrium. The letters of first separation are a progressive elaboration of illness, of the perception and vision of madness, but also the progressive clarification of it by the mind. As heroic combativeness gives letters the shape of a series of essential testings, the spiritual drama is only the Corneillian promontory above what La Rochefoucauld called "the uncharted regions of the map of self-love."

Numerous treatises on melancholy, had they been needed, among others Cureau de La Chambre's *On Tears, Fear, Despair*—into a fourth printing in 1662—could have offered full description of the state of dejection and withdrawal experienced in February 1671 and then accepted as a permanent danger with which mother and daughter had to live. The practical Marquise treated herself. She consulted able physicians, among them the distinguished Pecquet, and took medications. Among many the famous nostrum Queen of Hungary Water, thought to reduce acidity and restore spirits to true function, is "good against sadness," she confirms, tipsy from it (10.16.75). Light diet, fresh air, and brisk walking cool the blood, and chocolate for its contrary effect becomes an "enemy." Purges are taken monthly; bleeding, as last resort, regulates effusion of blood to the brain, thought one cause of derangement.

The mother was equally practical and perspicacious in treating the mind, aberrations, she saw, caused by feelings of sadness and dejection, unreasonable isolation and abandonment. The anxiety of a mother's excitable suggestibility, she diagnoses clairvoyantly— "What I suffer is in relation to you, not at all by your doing" (3.18.71). The best treatment is diversion. "I chase after distractions, the only remedy, often needed. . . . Your brother is a treasury of folly. . . . His wits are sometimes fricasseed in whipped cream, but otherwise he is lovable" (6.7.71). The remedy—in fact, the only one, and often needed, seen, and regulated by the wisdom gained through introspection in letters—is correspondence—"I must console myself and divert myself by writing to you" (2.20.71).

Of private words fashioned to describe anxiety and its symptoms, "stews," rambling (*radoterie*), childish babble (*lanternes*), the childlike "dragons" with its rich iconographic suggestiveness most suits the letter-writer. The dragons seem to assume a life of their own, creating scenes and the shape or shapelessness of letters. In response to a scene of reassuring endearment from Mme de Grignan, they dictate another, in which the often repeated word *folie* invokes a moment of self-induced hysteria. "You say you would like to see me come into your room and hear me talking. Alas! It is my *folie* to see you, to talk to you, to hear you. I am consumed by that desire and the pain of not having listened enough to you, of not having looked enough at you. It seems to me I scarcely lost a moment then, but I am not satisfied" (3.18.71). Passion and *folie* linked in the body of the letter also close it; reason is sacrificed. "Love my tenderness, love my weakness; I can very well live with them; I much prefer them to the thoughts of Seneca and Epictetus. I am mild and tender, my dear child, to the point of *folie*. You are everything to me; I know only you." "I am *folle*, nothing is truer, but you must love my *folie*. I do not understand how one can think so much of another. Will I never have thought it all? No, only when I think no more." Ultimately powerless, the mind struggles as it can to catch hold of experience.

Most scandalous to the letter-writer's mind, more so than its limitation and the power of an imagination turned "sorcerer" with a will to possession, is a pervasive sense of regression. "Shall I tell you I love you?" she asks in one closing. The question, which might open a love poem, is answered by a terse statement of self-blame cutting short any lyrical expansion—"It is ridiculous to be still at that stage" (3.13.71). But once again on the eighteenth she gave in: "Alas what would I not give to see into your heart, that place where I long to be," as she had on the eleventh: "I spend my life talking about you. . . . I don't see the slightest thing in your heart and imagine all sorts of troubling things."

In the explosions caused by failure of the post to yield letters from Provence, it becomes evident that Mme de Sévigné realizes the private world of her dragons threatens to enclose her and deals with them. She watches with alarm her vaunted spontaneity become uncontrollable impulse, obsessive repetition, verbal excess—punning (as far as the Passion even on March 26), mannerism, disconnected chronicling. Formulas once disdained in epistolary style are now insistently "the truth not just words." Most distressing among compulsive ritual precautions against anxiety are the length and number of letters. This too is *folie*, of a different sort, "foolishness" demanding control.

By the time of the second journey to Sainte-Marie, recounted (1.29.72) a week before the first anniversary of separation and headed "first rambling," art triumphs over the raw experience transcribed a year earlier. The scene of the mother alone in the convent garden, "where I have seen you a hundred times," is restrained; the letter, carefully closed with a successful testing of weakness, which replaces a final shaping paradox of unreason by resignation "in beauty." Even darkened by recent deaths and a somber account of the Princesse de Conti's last ordeal, the anniversary letter itself (2.5), headed "the day I was born a thousand years ago," manages a final smile, the appropriate gesture of acceptance of a fact now implying no grim destiny—"life itself is not dearer or more necessary than your affection."

First description of perilous balance remains nonetheless true, progress toward equilibrium never being uniform or fully stable. "There are days, hours, moments when I am not mistress of myself. I am weak and don't pride myself on being otherwise" (1.29.72) echoes that earlier less controlled moment: "For the moment I am quite reasonable. I do what I must to keep going and am sometimes four or five hours like anyone else. But a little thing causes me to regress. A memory, a place, a word, a thought too fixed, your letters especially, mine even while writing them, someone's speaking of you—all those things are reefs for my constancy upon which I often run aground" (2.18.71). Always true too is the essential message of that letter: "I am dying from the desire to know about you. As soon as I have a letter, I want another; I breathe only through them." No one better understood La Rochefoucauld's maxim later discussed with Mme de Grignan, "We have not strength enough to follow all our reason" (42), or in struggling for the whole picture the discouragement of his skeptical reflection: "To know things well, detail must be known, and since detail is almost infinite, our knowledge remains superficial and imperfect" (106).

As the life of the letters to Mme de Grignan unfolds, a special reality is imposed by dissociation of meanings of *folie*, at first purposely ambiguous, and by insistence on the metaphor of illness as the reality of a life without defense of joy or safeguards of reason. *Folie* as fancy is the whimsical and vivifying delight of civilized life, the movable feast in which language bids to games with it; Corneille's grandeur to exaltation; society's festivities and fashions, parades of ambition and foibles, to amusement and reflection; the trick perspectives and shaded bowers of gardens to refreshment and fantasy.

Defending the wisdom of this folly as a way of life becomes the business of the letters. Recognizing special truth in La Roche-foucauld's paradoxical maxim "He who lives without folly is not so wise as he thinks" (209), Mme de Sévigné defends it: "Alas! how can one live without folly, without fantasy that is?" (2.10.72). But when respect is entreated for *folie*, it is akin to the poet's ecstatic inspiration and becomes a part of the exalted language of love, flashes of imagination cutting the knotty reasoning of epistolary conversation. Different from verse quoted to ornament, beyond poets' swooning, this personally charged language opens onto *folie* that is darkening alienation of mind, kept distinct by a clinical physicality (breathing, sleep, "life as a dream," distorted vision, vapors, weariness, troubled concentration).

Intensified reality emerges as it does when a reader passes from the delusions of Virginia Woolf's Septimus Smith (in *Mrs. Dalloway*) to passages in letters and journal revealing material transformed in her fiction, the distorted perceptions Virginia Woolf herself felt as prelude to insanity. For Mme de Grignan, fiction and journal, poetry and physiology, emotion's compelling images and the mind's battle for control are made to coexist in her mother's letters.

II *First Reunions*

With renewed sense of function, as the Grignans' ambassador, adviser, and entertainer, Mme de Sévigné energetically relaunched herself into society. Reanimating all the qualities prose portraits had celebrated, with fine tact and the instincts of a skillful novelist, she brought the society to life in letters bursting with abbreviated scenarios, which hit every classification of life Balzac established to coordinate the fictional world of his *Human Comedy*. Unclad introspection and high sacrifice, as solicitations of reciprocal revelations of "hidden treasures" may effect a "reunion," but sustaining them is risky. "To tell you always that I love you, think only of you, am occupied only by what touches you, that you are the charm of my life, that no one was ever loved so dearly would distress you by repetition" (2.20.71). Long before first reunion in Provence, thought, imagination, and the epistolary skill of the letters on Foucquet, to Bussy and Grignan, had found other ways. As the letter-writer's mind is challenged and regains balance it more than makes do with elusive symbolic reunions of epistolary conversation. Recreated with every distinctive nuance of mixed tones and random associative movement Mme de Grignan remembered and missed, that conversation has all the old freedom and sharpness Bussy found in the daughter's conversation as well as her mother's and laughter rich enough to challenge Balzac's theory that one of its sounds is the key to characterization.

Each time Mme de Sévigné crosses her threshold, for Court or to seek favor of ministers, bishops or judges, for public functions or evenings with old friends, on errands or with relatives, Mme de Grignan is taken with her. "As soon as I hear anything fine, I wish for you. You have a part in everything I think" (2.27.71) is the promise faithfully kept in letters. "Provisions" or an "hors-d'œuvre," she laughed, are stocked for the special but familiar feasts of conversation. They follow as surely as had formerly direct commentary on events, or books, with the pleasures of family wit and the private language of mother and daughter. Code names—

the Great Man (Louis XIV), Quanto (Montespan), Charming (Villeroy), Rain (Pomponne)—are not prudent cryptonyms for inspectors, free to open all publicly conveyed mail but powerless to curb the Marquise's virtual freedoms in epistolary conversations. Like "dragons" and pet endearments, the figures of Italian romance and *commedia dell'arte*, pastoral verse, ballet and opera, they maintain a continuing game of the private language and a part of its sustained illusion. Similarly, regularly recurrent references to her "old disorderly style" do not reflect abstract critical thought on epistolary style so much as name and confirm the illusion they serve.[7]

With each bit of information from Provence, Mme de Sévigné first strives to see her daughter in its new light—"Write about you," she requests directly, then strains her imagination to visualize a scene in which she may in turn walk out with Mme de Grignan. "I prefer to occupy myself with your new life; doing so diverts me without distraction from my subject and object, which poets call the loved one" (3.3.71). Others are pressed into service. From relatives and family friends, less known travelers, servants, all quoted back to Mme de Grignan, the mother continues her composite picture, it like those accounts "never finishing on your beauty, your civility, your wit, your capability, and even the coiffure you manage as though in the midst of court society" (6.10.71).

"Nothing is lost on me," the letter-writer affirms, again quoting Bussy's jab at her, significantly relocating old conversational pleasures and at the same time refining a new style that transforms the old manner. Banter yet permits itself old privileges and strategic advantages, juxtaposed with the spiritual drama. "Scoundrel, why do you sometimes conceal precious treasures? Do you fear I may die from joy? Don't you fear I may die from grief believing the contrary?" (2.18.71). The new epistolary style others (Coulanges, Bussy, and Grignan, notably)[8] saw as a "style of affection." Mme de Sévigné herself felt it more fully as the style of perfect friendship, and as its first maxim she insists: "The slightest details are as precious from those loved perfectly as they are tiresome from others, as we have said a thousand times" (3.13.71). It is not surprising that Mme de Grignan's style is first praised in detail, as Bussy had her mother's, for its naturalness, and for its distinctively expressive "noble simplicity." Happy that her daughter's letters

had nothing of the formulas of "five-penny" commercial secretaries ("saddles for all horses") or of officialdom, or the "fly-
tracks" of fashionable young women whose letters convey less
maturity than Françoise-Marguerite's at ten, she wrote: "Never
stop being natural; your turn of phrase has been formed by being
so, and that naturalness constitutes a perfect style" (2.11; 18.71).
No abstract canon of taste or style is brought to bear. The style is
perfect because it satisfies the mother's desires for information and
communication. The perfect letter, for both correspondents but
especially Mme de Sévigné, is and will remain despite all its risks a
perfect transparency.

Wherever the scenes of symbolic reunion are that rapidly inter-
play within letters, their center is the theater of memory brought to
life in the present. Those passing pleasures of a mother's familiar
conversation, carefully modulated and imaginatively maintained,
become the heart of letters and regulate the function of their parts.

Time itself is the first concern. Again practical, Mme de Sévigné
watched vigilantly over the post, its ordinary delay of five days
after leaving Paris for Aix on Wednesday and Friday evenings and
delivery at Grignan on the sixth, and the hazards that further
delayed it as her first letters were—foul weather, bad roads, delayed relays, limitations of horses and couriers running only during
the day. Depending entirely on public service, she cultivated a
"little friend" in the post, occasionally jostled the minister responsible for it, made personal calls with letters (time to add a last
word). The disorders of the post become a principal theme, no
purely literary one, as postal rhythms are adapted to the letter-
writer's advantage and modify her style. "When we are far apart
we no longer mock letters beginning 'I received yours of the, etc.' "
(2.11.71), she gladly conceded, with concern quoted by the narrator
of Proust's *The Captive*.[9] Her own letters invariably begin with
those notations, anxiously desired in return from Mme de Grignan
as assurance of fixed points of dialogue and insurance against the
horror of the "wrong card turned up at the wrong moment."
Within letters time was tamed in other ways.

Very soon ritual hours were set aside to be alone with letter-
writing, first in the rue de Thorigny and then a new house in the rue
de Trois-Pavillons, leased and fitted out "only with the hope of
seeing you there," Mme de Sévigné wrote, assuring the continuity
of old dreams (4.29; 5.4.72). The mother gilded the schedule,

fundamentally a protective measure of structuring habit. "I shall be punctual because of the pleasure I take in writing, not for punctuality's sake" (3.18.71). By mid-March the background image of the writer fixed with the habit is a scene ordinarily of quiet pleasure, shatterable, she demonstrates, only by extraordinary circumstances. Typically, the setting of the scene (3.13.71) is followed by news, then turns inward to reminiscence—the mother and daughter in devotion—that recreates the past. "Here I am with a joyful heart, alone in my room writing peacefully to you. Nothing is so agreeable for me. I dined with Mme de Lavardin, after Bourdalouing, where I saw the Mothers of the Church, as I call the Princesses de Conti and de Longueville. Everyone was there . . . you would have . . . and I would have. . . ."

The pattern is repeated. "M. de La Rochefoucauld received your compliment with great pleasure at the Lavardins, where you are much spoken of. M. d'Ambres was there with his cousin Mme de Brissac and seemed much interested in your near shipwreck. Your bravery was spoken of, and M. de La Rochefoucauld remarked that you wanted to appear brave. . . ." News of a fair visited follows, followed again by the account of a visit to the Hôtel de Rambouillet. Frank laughter from the fair is mingled with the refined amusement over La Rochefoucauld's typical manner of turning a maxim and also nostalgic gaiety at the Hôtel—a second intimate scene of reminiscence—"I make myself laugh seeing the pleasure all this gave me."

More laughter and different tones are added as news of the Court brings an anecdote of Mme de Ludres's being bitten by a mad dog. As the letter-writer plays maliciously with the anecdote, and on the poet Benserade's distress, Mme de Ludres is costumed as Andromeda. The grotesque incongruity of the imposed cure, bathing naked in the sea, is flashed up and crowned by a pastiche of her Germanic accent that gives distress the sound of the comic Swiss in Molière's *Pourceaugnac*. On the crest of mirth comes a poke at the marriage of Mlle d'Houdancourt and the Duc de Ventadour with vintage Rabutin ribaldry.

All this news and amusement, reflects the letter-writer, becoming serious, is so much babble. "You believe I conjure up what you are doing," she begins a third scene that would shift reunion to Provence. But it must be cut short for want of information and ends with the first maxim of the new letter-writing, which makes it

possible: "The slightest details are precious. . . .," more precious
of course than anything at Rambouillet or elsewhere.

Two paragraphs of assorted domestic news bring concern for her
son and an unusual, cool reference to her husband: "Your brother
begins to be under the laws of Ninon, which I doubt will be good
for him. They don't profit some minds. She spoiled your father.
Your brother must be left to God, but when one is a Christian, or
has the will to be, seeing these disorders is painful." This intimate
confidence of one woman to another is followed by a fourth rapprochement, through Mme de Grignan's often mentioned portrait.
A copy has been given to Mme de Lafayette and decorates another
room where its subject "is never forgotten."

All this leads to the final question, the fear of regression already
quoted—"Shall I tell you I love you?" and a conclusion "in
beauty"—"As I am delighted when you assure me of your tenderness, I assure you of mine, to give you joy if you are in my humor."
A last turn catches old banter. "And that Grignan, does he merit a
word?" In closing there is also an exhortation to seek continuity in
the life of the letters, playing against a last intimate memory of
Mme de Grignan's keeping her mother's letters as a girl—"If you
are still disposed as you were at Sainte-Marie to keep my letters, see
if you still have February 18th's."

This relatively short letter of March 13 epitomizes the art of the
new letter-writing in "normal" circumstances, its diversity, the
unity within diversity (what Pascal sought by a technique of suffu-
sion, "attention to every detail by reference to its end"), the
permanent tensions of tones, scenes, emotions. Tension is maintained between solitary calm and the outside world, its time and the
present inner time of joyously detailed chronicle; likewise, it exists
between the "only subject and object," between Mme de Grignan
and others who are distractions—"loving you makes me find all
other loves frivolous" (3.18.71). The illusion is that son, son-in-
law, granddaughter also "sacrificed" in the special truth of a
closing (3.11.71) do not matter. Elements of the old style, gossip
and chronicle, compliment and hyperbole, banter, all there but
insistently different, remain also in tension with the new style of
perfect friendship.

"Don't think that compliments and treating me like the *Holland
Gazette* will placate me; I'll have my revenge" (3.11.71), the
Parisian correspondent threatens when informed that one of her

letters has been read out, sure of having demonstrated the truths
that her unique correspondent is the exclusive audience sought and
her only "good news." At first news stands apart, society gazettes
adrift on separate pages, caught on the run, with frantic expense of
movement and grappling with time, as though letters translated
literally her desire "I like to talk with you [i.e., to write] at any
hour" (3.3.71) or La Rochefoucauld's observation: "Love like fire
cannot subsist without perpetual movement" (75). Letters are
begun or finished at the Coulanges', with La Rochefoucauld or
Mme de Lafayette, Charles or Mme de La Troche, anywhere it
seems, with messages from everyone. Succumbing to the illusion,
caricaturists have delighted to picture the Marquise hard at her
writing in unlikely places. But the scenes of writing at home, the
private and ritualized pleasures, in spring and summer (but not
because of the seasons, she assures) coordinate the message more
subtly. Time signatures fix the structure of days, confirming that
Mme de Grignan is first and last in her mother's mind, and on
installments link days by the continuity of her daughter's presence.
You are my time, as loving you is the substance of life, is the
message conveyed, personal profession of La Rochefoucauld's
generalization—"the duration of our passions is no more dependent on us than the duration of our lives" (5).

As news makes its way into the body of letters, one more re-
minder of the reality of "habitual thought," the letter-writer
becomes the avowed "enemy of false news" (5.4.72) who insists "I
invent nothing" (7.16.72). Forwarding the real gazettes, she dis-
penses her letters from a "Renaudot style" (4.10; 10.21.71) in com-
petition with them.[10] Compliments spun off on impulse merge with
news in more thoughtful proofs of habitual thought. Projecting
sadness and giving old gallantry its way, the letter-writer had
written "the Mardi Gras ball was all but suspended; never was
there such a sad affair. I believe your absence was the cause." Fore-
stalling teasing or worse, endangered credibility, since the *Gazette*
reported "the most brilliant and beautiful of masquerades,"[11]
irony is subsequently accentuated, as it usually is when old banter
appears. "I must say with Voiture 'No one has yet died of your
absence but me.' I believed the ball was sad because of your absence, but that sadness is not enough to express absence like yours"
(2.18.71). The metaphor remains, as does the gloss's directness,
transformed by more simply expressed tenderness of reminiscence.

Told by the Duc d'Orléans that she should not miss a ball because of her daughter's absence, Mme de Sévigné reports her wish to miss it precisely for that reason (1.22.72). The only balls desired are those in which Mlle de Sévigné dances, remembered with quiet pleasure at Les Rochers.

Some of Mme de Sévigné's most famous sustained descriptions, "relation"-letters, like the more detailed letter-journals of introspection, owe their beginnings to rhythms as well as disorders of the post. The necessity of finding her subject within herself, of being drawn inward until effort of mind seeks distractions, caused by delayed delivery, becomes in the new order of things a weekly event. The first letter of the week begins as a close commentary of Mme de Grignan's letters (received on Monday and Wednesday), going where it will from there. But the second usually shorter letter "on the head of a pin" had to find its own beginnings and developments, "on whatever comes to mind," since new letters from Provence arrived only after its scheduled departure on Friday evening.[12] Both order and disorder of the post, as much as any pleasure of self-expression, sharpened the art of the style of perfect friendship and when most needed its communication of the illusion of "reunion." All Paris and the Court, family and friends, at those moments seem fair game for the drama and wit that recapture intimacy in conversation.

The first "relation," reporting a fire at night in the Guitauts' neighboring house, came at a moment when delayed mail and anxiety made the consolation of writing a boon of illusory nearness (2.20.71). The description opens with the letter-writer abruptly awakened to danger, a moment of half-consciousness that metaphorically parallels the mother's first anxious nights. Rapid narration of events, hurrying her to the center of the scene, preserves the air of unreality as familiar street and figures appear in the unnatural light of the fire and are quickened by peril. Danger past, narration is relaxed; as mother and daughter might have done in the safety of their rooms, the letter-writer enjoys humorous incongruity. "Could we have laughed, what portraits we made! Guitaut was naked except for nightshirt and shoes. Mme de Guitaut was barelegged and with one slipper. Mme de Vauvineux was in full petticoat without a dressing gown. All the valets and neighbors were in nightcaps. The Venetian ambassador had on his dressing gown and great wig and the full gravity of his ambassadorship. But his secretary! The chest of a Hercules! Truly! It was entirely visible, white, thick, fleshy, exposed by a lost fastening." As all the night's dangers, real and metaphorical, are dispelled, the mother's mind associating freely on water's effects moves from humor to final quiet intimacy. "I hope, my *bonne*, the water you are taking is doing you good. In a word, I wish you everything and pray God keep you from all harm."

A grandiose scene is articulated in the same manner. The famous description of the commemoration at the Oratory of Séguier's death (5.6.72) seems to have all the pomp and solemnity of tone befitting the subject, the setting by Le Brun, and the attention of the Grignans. Accordingly old sarcasm has vanished with the fact of Séguier's death "like a great man" (2.3.72). But seeing with Mme de Grignan's eyes, tastes, and wit every detail up to final turns of wit and tenderness, the letter-writer shapes a letter more for her daughter than about Séguier. Rapprochement is effected at every point. From her place in the Oratory, nearer Bishop Mascaron (sought out because from Provence) than she is to Colbert, her eye is struck by the Duke of Monmouth (handsome as ever, she confides). After raising her eyes to appreciate the "masterpiece of Le Brun," they are closed in pleasures of the music, in communion with the musical Grignans, to whom the "inexplicable beauty" of Lully's *Miserere* would also seem "the apogee of all the King's music." The cynosure of all eyes and the letter is the young priest, obviously nervous to offer his eulogy in the intimidating setting. Having learned from Mascaron's whisper that he is the Bishop's protégé and from Marseilles, Mme de Sévigné's imagination is fixed by his southern accent and gives her all Provence. The unusually detailed description of his successful testing becomes in effect the triumph of Provence.

As she leaves, the letter-writer reports conspiratorial laughter, shared with Guitaut as it would have been with her daughter. Failing to spot her old friend Forbin-Janson, the Bishop of Marseilles who was complicating the Grignans' lives and elsewhere is baptized "Hail," she retorted with malicious incongruity: "If this had been the funeral of somebody living you can bet he would be here." "But I am silly, what can such a lengthy narration serve?" the letter-writer reflects on the indulgent consolation of closeness writing has given. Humor, breaking a solemn scene as unexpectedly as the Maréchal de Gramont's expostulation, replaces meditation on death that might follow in a set-piece and again leads the mind by association to final tender reminiscence. Guitaut's presence brings to mind a letter to him from Mme de Grignan, the only text needed for meditation at the moment of withdrawal from the letter and the passionately awaited but delayed departure for Provence: "Send my mother to me," she had written.

Malicious wit like Rabutin raciness flickers through the early letters, more than later, with physical ugliness, awkwardness or stupidity, derided as openly as their opposites are freely enjoyed. Like other collectors the letter-writer repeats Mme Cornuel's acid sayings, but she prefers her own. Suspending in an anecdote the "bony hand" of Mme de Gêvres, in mid-air as it reaches out unsuccessfully to usurp a precedence of the Duchesse d'Arpajon, she admits "I am malicious, it cheers me" (3.30.71). For the most part this vengeful laughter of ridicule, here in the cause of a good friend, is another feature of the new style of perfect friendship. Mme de Grignan's enemies are her mother's, Forbin-Janson coming in for his share of the raillery that punishes others who have not always been the daughter's friends. The Comtesse de Marans, dubbed "Mélusine" permanently, is for example repaid for vicious gossip. She is caught out in grotesque devotion, as incongruous and modish as her "haystack" coiffure, the picture of the "placard springtime of a country inn." Mme de Lafayette is allowed the *coup de grâce*; "You are entirely ridiculous," she confronted the hapless figure with bluntness the Sévignés did not always find easy to take. That Mme de Grignan particularly enjoyed this kind of wit her mother knew and occasionally administers mild motherly chiding. But in the new letter-writing she found it no hanging matter. The indulgent mother is however never led to "sacrifice" Mme de Lafayette; when insinuations about that other old friendship must be answered, the pen is left to Charles.

In the new pleasures of ridiculing everything deserving it, Mme de Sévigné warms herself most often with humor engaged by temperamental and intellectual affinity with Molière's comedy. "If Molière were here," introduces her own continuations of his comic spirit before and after his death. Tagnames (a Tartuffe, an Agnes or a Cathos) and lines recalled from speeches, of an ungainly lover (Arnolphe of *The School for Wives*), or preposterous display of knowledge (Sganarelle of *The Doctor in Spite of Himself*) abound from knowledge of all the plays.[13] They are so many comic masks and directorial gestures for offstage actors and scenes of farce. But the affinity goes deeper to tap the comic principle of the "incongruous," the aesthetics of comedy sketched in the *Letter on the Impostor* (1667), Molière's response to the critics of *Tartuffe*. "Ridiculous" seems to appear on every page of the letters. For the two correspondents, sharing Mme de Sévigné's distaste and amusement over "bad copies of better originals," both the principle and the symptoms set in the *Letter* offer comedy as diverse as Molière's own.

The ridiculous is the outward and visible form that nature's providence has fixed to all that is contrary to reason, in order to make us avoid it. To appreciate it, we must appreciate that reasonable quality of which it suggests the lack and perceive what constitutes the quality . . . the essence of the ridiculous is incongruity . . . thence it follows that all lying, disguising, cheating, dissimulation, any outward show different from the underlying reality, in short any contradiction between actions arising from the same principle, is essentially ridiculous.[14]

Perceiving her own special reason of style—"It is a pleasure to send you pretty things, you respond so deliciously" (3.23.71)—as well as the reason of heroic testing, introspection, practicality, and health, the letter-writer allows free reign to comic imagination, as vital as any other structure of reason in answering the demands upon correspondents and letter-writing. Potentially importunate maternal advice and many a cautionary tale on matters of concern at Grignan—up-to-date fashion and proper protocol, gambling and lavish display, pregnancy—are shielded and made eloquent by comic vision. Its expression, not limited to laughter, enlists allegorical personification, satire, romanesque and pastoral fictions. A striking example in the matter of extravagant display is her most famous "relation," of the chef Vatel's incongruous suicide after the dishonor of a ruined dinner sumptuously planned for the King's visit to Chantilly. Beyond careful private documentation and finely restrained dramatic narration, fully restored for the first by Duchêne's texts (4.24; 26.71), lies a moralist's point of view—all in vain—with irony eloquently cautionary for the Grignans. Seeking to match the King in grandeur or to dazzle him by it is essentially ridiculous, an axiomatic truth learned from experience. Then, too, the

King may be a "hero for all seasons," his "courtiers are woebegone, without a sou" (12.23.71).

On the principle of incongruity turn portraits and raillery, anecdotes, sustained narrations from Foucquet's trial to Guitaut's fire and Séguier's funeral, as unexpectedly unfitting speech, gestures, and events tease an alert sense of comedy and delight with easy or thoughtful laughter. Without direct sentimentality or moralizing, eccentricities and oddities, awkward performances and misshapen expressions are gathered as enthusiastically as Charles's treasury of follies, and comic silhouettes are set into motion. The absentminded family friend, the Comte de Brancas, a model later for La Bruyère's Theophrastian character of the distracted man (Ménalque), like many others is sent careening and misspeaking himself through the letters to the mirth of the correspondents. So too is a deaf and vague cousin, Mlle de Méri, until her puzzling afflictions become too painful to watch (11.24.79). The miseries and upheavals of domestic life are generally relieved by comedy. Amid nurses and infant medications for her granddaughter the letter-writer laughs herself into "Pourceaugnac's apothecary shop," and embroiled by Charles's first gallantries she manages again with scenes of her own Moliéresque comedy.

Humming the lingering comic motif "Little brother goes a courting," once the dangers of his three-week fiasco with Ninon are past, domestic drama for the amusement of Mme de Grignan is made a comic spectacle of clumsy romancing. Three times at least there is hearty laughter over Ninon's *bon mot*, indiscreetly confided by Charles and touching off ridicule, that he has "the heart of a melon fricasseed in snow." Breaking anxieties about daughter as well as son, as she does in the sustained descriptions, the letter-writer reports conspiratorial laughter shared by mother and son, and La Rochefoucauld, that now includes Mme de Grignan. With Charles's further indiscreet disclosures, of failure to consummate an affair with the actress La Champmeslé and debaucheries in the company of Boileau among others, another scene follows "worthy of Molière" (4.8.71) or Petronius, as Charles distressedly contemplates Pecquet's treatment, then dreams aloud of impotence (4.17). Wit drains poison from the impotence and the son's recrimination, that his mother's "ice" would better have been inherited by Mme de Grignan (again pregnant?). Sympathetic concern for Charles remains, as in more serious later casualties of gallantry, but the reason of folly is obscured by the illusion of "sacrifice" of son to daughter. "What Mme de Sévigné felt for her daughter can more justly be likened to the passion depicted by Racine in *Andromaque* and *Phèdre* than can the banal relations of the young Sévigné with his mistress," argues Proust's Charlus (I, 763). Of all the gifts of comic vision, whose ridicule never touches that love—or Mme de Grignan's for her husband ("we have similar symptoms," she continued to feel), the greatest comes in summer and autumn at Les Rochers, in the stabilizing letters of the letter-writer's private "Scenes of Life in the Provinces."

III *Traveling*

The letters of 1671 are unique among all the series that follow them from Les Rochers. They have a freshness of open air, a relaxed playfulness, and special consolations not duplicated exactly in later years. As the mother walks through her trees, she finds there memories of her daughter's companionship and of her childhood games, which keep "black chagrin" a poignant motif. But her vivid imagination does not make of the woods a labyrinth of dark thought (7.29), even as autumn or winter approached, while walking at the favorite hour of twilight (8.23), or quoting verse from a woodland shelter (7.19) that becomes the new scene of ritual letter-writing. Afternoons with Tasso's poetry, Molière and Rabelais read aloud by Charles, Corneille, biographies and some history are refreshing dips into the past. "I am like Don Quixote," she laughed with the novels of her youth (8.9). New moral essays by Nicole "of the same cloth as Pascal" are mentioned at intervals, discussed briefly in the autumn (9.30), but do not weigh on the life of the letters. Brief also are death notices, even of old friends like Lenet. Nor does vigorous description of rustic life carry the burden of echoes of the Roman poet Horace's praise of happy country life, commonplaces of education seemingly inescapable for men of letters in holidays or exile from Paris.

"Blackness" most often has material causes, at once imaginative and concrete pictures of rural life, which fills time but not the mind, could be and was often fatiguing and boring. Business made necessary periodical trips to Brittany, long since felt as self-imposed exile by the Marquise. Long before 1671, the Marquise's letters had made of necessity virtues of holiday and retreat. In 1671 days of rain (and letters like them), unwelcome callers, routines of estate business and society expected of the visiting châteleine give a new, fully exploited literalness to the consolation felt and celebrated afresh in the correspondence of mother and daughter. Continuity with its past is maintained with an apparent effortlessness that makes scrupulous repetitions and translations of the tensions of the style of perfect friendship, epitomized in the letter of March 13, seem all the more natural.

All the baggage needed, mother assured daughter, is the un-changing image of Mme de Grignan's portrait (5.23), kept with new images of the most recent letters in her pocket as in her heart. Thus fortified, preparations can be faced with a light heart. The Marquise cannot resist a smile as she sets her two calèches into motion, with their contents of maids and the dog Marphise, the Abbés La Mousse (Mme de Grignan's former tutor, who taught her Cartesian principles among other things) and de Coulanges reading their breviaries—but rusty at the Mass, she later jokes—while the Marquise and Charles read from "their breviary of Corneille." As it must have done when Mlle de Sévigné was a part of it, the spec-tacle and hubbub suggest a troop of traveling players embarking on a tour of the provinces. Luckily, with the traveler also went the past of the correspondence and its momentum of effort, satisfactions, and hopes. Two months before arrival in Brittany Mme de Sévigné had begun to worry, about the changed image of herself Brittany would give to her letters and its effects on correspondence. "What can I write to you about from my woods?" she fretted. Without Paris, the mother risked losing the new functions, of informant, intermediary, entertainer, reconstructed by the letter-writer. Adding distance to separation, "absence to absence" (3.23), seemed absurdly like adding a measure to infinity. Changed postal routes spelled trouble. New subjects for letter-writing threatened to be so much dead weight of banality of the weather. But as Mme de Grignan's image remains unchanged in her letters, as her renewed first promise of understanding responsiveness to new problems (5.6.71) materializes in them, problems subside one by one for the letter-writer. Mme de Sévigné begins to enjoy her art with a new ease and through it to find new strength in the circumstances of a new testing.

Traveling on the promise alone, the letter-writer sets the tone

that gives continuity and coherence to the first letters from Brittany. The letters in preparation, from Malicorne while traveling,
and on arrival, are a tested mixture of tenderness, light comedy,
and pastoral, practical detail and personal information. Shaped by
the mother's desire "to give you something pretty, you respond so
deliciously," they frame the exile from Paris and master the new
distance from Provence by an almost unbroken series of privately
meaningful gifts exchanged by mother and daughter.

Traveling with Mme de Sévigné has long delighted readers who
follow her to the garden of Livry or the Burgundian fields of Bourbilly, along the leisurely Loire or by coach to Brittany. Horace
Walpole followed "His Lady of the Rocks," as Lamartine did
later, to the woods of Les Rochers. Descriptions of the woods and
rustic life, to which they are the gateway in the letters, are not in
themselves elaborate. Brief notations of place, qualified mostly by
abstract adjectives ("beautiful," "fresh," often) and given an hour
and its lighting, provide a setting, with a tactile sense of materiality
painters may offer by clear lines of perspective. Impressions and
associations, by spontaneous play of senses and mind, animate the
setting, capture then share scenes as metaphors of a familiar past.
Letter-travelogues imagined or written en route, as Mme de
Grignan had, in 1671 and later more elaborately function much like
those scenes. In whatever conveyance, the correspondent is taken
along its route; by a pace of writing suggesting its motion and by a
roving eye, made a companion to pleasures, first of movement and
changing scene, then of confiding memory awakened by them. As
physical distance increases, then reaches its limit, those letters
reduce it by a constant of intimacy, invariable no matter what
factors of velocity or distance.

To Mme de Grignan the "adoration of the lovable freedom of
Les Rochers" in 1671 is communicated as fully as was from Paris
the physical reality of the trauma and confinement of first separation. Again walking to make up for time shut in her room, the
letter-writer finds release from its confines she had not found at
Livry. Now, walks at all hours, the sights of new earth and crops
(7.22), tastes of chestnuts and country butter, the feeling of her
workers in the fields (6.28) or of surprise visits, all build an illusion
of sensual joy that sustains the first pleasures of newness on arrival,
preserved and refined by the letter-writer.

From Mme de Grignan came the cues that set the controlling metaphors of the familiar past, games of Mlle de Sévigné's childhood and the comedy of provincial life that mother and daughter had shared as one of those games. They are tenderly evoked as the mother plays hide-and-seek with memory and tumultuously prolongs games with new scenes whose comic mischief tumbles through the summer.

"You would like, you say, to leave your splendor and be a simple shepherdess with me in my woods," Mme de Sévigné muses on her daughter's first responsive understanding of the perils of new separation. Neither correspondent indulged in literary games of pastiche of pastoral style. Literary reminiscence, as always, enhances or crystallizes reality, which is the bond of familiar memory. Finding on arrival mottoes on trees, which continue a motif of D'Urfé's pastoral romance *L'Astrée*, it is a game played by the younger Sévignés that is recalled. Lessons "out of school" are offered in Italian, which the mother wishes to keep fresh in her daughter's mind, or in an echo of La Fontaine ("I am astounded to hear trees and fountains speak") that continues with good humor a running disagreement of mother and daughter on the refreshment he offers to the mind. A letter addressed to Mme de Grignan "At the Château of Apollidon" is followed in the same spirit of imaginative "reunion" by one sent back "to the shelter (*capucine*) in the woods of Les Rochers." Extending the game, the mother sings the refrain her daughter had, "Alas when will the time come again, shepherdess?" wistfully when absence is felt, but offers with it counsel (refrain and counsel both expurgated by Perrin).

The texture of pastoral is broken by the realities of Grignan, in which the mother would play her continuing part. "Amuse yourself, don't worry needlessly, no depression, take your pregnancy to its term safely" (7.12). By Mme de Grignan's responses, the message of the woods is communicated, appreciated, reciprocated. "You invite me, *ma bonne*, to walk in your heart and you say a thousand lovable things of that place. So I shall tell you that I do take that walk, beautiful and most agreeable for me, but in the same spirit I invite you to walk here with me" (8.2). But the symbolic reunion remains just that, a walk in "my woods," where every letter begins or ends or longs to be, less satisfying than that anticipated at Grignan. Playing on La Mousse's Cartesian instruction, again "out of school," with the distinction of soul and body, the mother puts the game into perspective once and for all; the adversative conjunction "but" lurks always in her woods: "But, my Lord! [these walks] are not happiness; there are certain gross physical realities one cannot do without" (8.2).

Old friends unexpectedly appearing in the woods enlarge the audience for Mme de Grignan's new life as they had in Paris. New friends may be admitted to the private rituals as they prove themselves worthy witnesses to the special relationship of mother and daughter. "I found the dialogue you wrote one day with Pommenars; we laughed ourselves to tears" (6.24). The rogue Pommenars, fleeing from arrest half-heartedly, diverts the Marquise with his insouciant wit but even more by his resurrection of the past game, both repeated to delight her daughter. Then one day Pommenars brings the Duchesse de Chaulnes, wife of the governor of Brittany. She bursts into the room in hunting costume, announced only by gales of laughter, infectiously prolonged for Mme de Grignan after the company retires (7.26). Bemused briefly by wealth and position[15] unfairly unlike Mme de Grignan's "destiny," the Marquise allows herself to be charmed entirely by the openness, generosity, and spontaneous unconventionality of Mme de Chaulnes, one of the few younger women made close friends after 1671 ("young women are silly, except one"). She is always the energy of the breathless scramble for shelter enjoyed by the two women with girlish exuberance on a rainy day at Les Rochers, a breath of the right kind of air to send to Grignan. But full friendship and that rightness are the reward of proper understanding: "Mme de Chaulnes says that she wishes a Mme de Sévigné for you in Provence like the one she has found here."

When a young gypsy, from a band happily sheltered for their unexpected diversion, dances for Mme de Sévigné, she is struck by the resemblance to her daughter and befriends the girl for that reason. In her long letter of friendship (6.28) the mother ended with the image of the dancing gypsy. The daughter may have responded with a gesture of tenderness worthy of her mother's first compliment on the "loved one's portrait." As a memorial to the letter, a new portrait was painted of Mme de Grignan in the costume of a gypsy.[16]

Anyone or anything obtruding on this privacy must beware. The Marquise keeps her distance by scenes staged and directed for her daughter's amusement, in the spirit of Molière's stiffly snobbish Sotenvilles (*George Dandin*), his clumsy country girls who would be Parisian ladies, or the new comedy of the gentry sketched in his *Comtesse d'Escarbagnas*. Impatient herself at being made a part of society the letter-writer mocks as "provincial repertory," she snobbishly resists being forced to play out her own comic metaphor of the traveling players. Continuing of course the "sacrifices" to perfect friendship, the mother compensates for loss of other functions by becoming an entertainer with a vengeance. Baiting and exposing the pretensions to style of a neighbor, Mlle Du Plessis D'Argentré, "Tartuffe in the flesh" (7.5), would have palled quickly as summer sport. But "slaps" administering lessons of style, that "the fine air of the court comes from its freedom from airs" (7.8), were also the prolongation of a real slap Mlle de Sévigné had dealt her childhood playmate. "Mimic her tone," as Mme de Sévigné herself continues to do, "and you would have given her a slap. . . . I wish you could hear her flatter and copy me. She also remembers things you said here, which she mouths back with the same grace. Alas! If there weren't better to make me remember you, I would be happy with even that" (6.7).

Mlle Du Plessis is only the beginning. The society of Brittany is leveled in a crescendo of scenes as mischievously as it is by the Marquise's running comic distortions of noneuphonious Breton names (Mlle Croak-Bird among the delights). With a child's peevishness over interrupted games, the letter-writer leaves starched callers in their carriage in the rain (6.28) or, when trapped, in silence in her drawingroom. With childlike unrepentance she tells the tale on herself of mistaking a local worthy for her host's butler (9.6). Hunger made her do it. The comic finale and the gift of August come with the Estates of Brittany, convened at Vitré for its yearly business that included ratification of gifts to the royal treasury and administrators (unfortunately more lavish than those the Grignans might expect in Provence). "All Brittany" threatened to invade her stage and privacy. The letters enlivened by the doings of the Estates, in which much meditation including the new resignation to tepid devotion finds place (Nos. 189-98), are fueled by typical delight in new experiences and in excess whether sublime or grotesque. Excess seems everywhere. Platters of fruit piled too high come tumbling down (8.5); civilities heaped ridiculously upon the Marquise court the same comic fate. Dancing is riotous (except once when finely executed it lives again with the memory of her daughter's past). Toasts are made to one and all until "all Brittany is intoxicated," including one Breton who jovially mistoasts "Mme de Carigan" for Mme de Grignan (8.19). Even as an institution the Estates seem absurdly out of proportion to the goings-on: "The Estates should not be long. The King's wish is their command. Said and done" (8.5)

Glad to return to her woods, happy there with an old friend who shares the memory of her daughter's celebration of its "wildness," Mme de Sévigné reexperiences the truth she found in her room in the rue de Thorigny and at Livry. "We feel more than ever that memory is in the heart" (9.9), she reaffirms, making the renewed games of the letter embody her truth, the old one of the only true consolation in absence. She had already apologized for indulgent pleasures (9.6) in the loved one's absence and made the case for the true pleasure of memory—"The Estates shouted in vain, danced and drank, your image (*idée*) remained always in its place" (9.2). The past to which the letter-writer turns is the past of the correspondence. Experience proves her prediction, not Mme de Grignan's, on "diversion" to be correct; the mother is diverted but not consoled: "As for me, I cannot become used to my daughter's being taken from me . . . you know I love you more than life" (9.9). As the mother promised—"What will console me for losing you? Nothing I've found could make that boast" (5.15). In the calm after introspection, the letter-writer closes with new confidence that matured with her summer. "You need only M. de Grignan and yourself" (9.13).

Satisfied by her daughter's appreciation of the mother's special tenderness and reciprocation of it, Mme de Sévigné wrote to her friend D'Hacqueville a letter (6.17.71) that gave the contrary impression. Its uncontrolled anxiety, about her daughter's silence, is more desperately expressed than any since the first letter of separation. Another letter now lost (not kept?) was written to her daughter on the same rainy Wednesday following the silence of three regular mail days. D'Hacqueville's letter, tactlessly forwarded to Grignan, triggered a real crisis. Both correspondents felt a breach of the privileged privacy of the correspondence. The letter reveals a doubt already implied by the preceding note's "thoughts La Rochefoucauld calls gray-brown" (6.14), which with the "rhapsody" before it (6.10) graphically represent the metaphor of troubled breathing when correspondence became irregular. "Love me. We have turned that expression to ridicule, but it is natural, it is good," the uncertain mother pleaded pathetically, too long after having written "You have written to me everywhere, which is done only from great friendship. I have marveled at your goodness" (2.18.71). Obsessive fear of an end to communication seems about to be reality.

Assured that Mme de Grignan was in fact alive, death having been the worst fear on June 17, normal epistolary respiration resumes—"Finally, my *bonne*, I breathe easily" (6.21). Relief as enormous as Arnolphe's "ouf," ending Molière's *The School for Wives*, allows the letter-writer to ridicule the anxious mother's performance. She gladly faces up to a public spectacle of her "habitual thought" she had more than once promised not to make (3.11.71). When Mme de Grignan's compassion follows first annoyance, the worst has been faced, allowing both women to weather a second, similar crisis in October and November. "How your belly weighs on me, suffocates me as it does you!" (10.21), the mother wrote, as she was now kept carefully abreast of a course of pregnancy that brings the letter-writer to a "safe term" of her own.

In October at Les Rochers, the first challenges of middle age seem to be felt (10.7). Demons appear that are not playful optical illusions of the woods at night (10.25). Strenuous exercise is sought (10.28); and in repose, there are new ruminations about the need for God's grace to crown strenuous self-demand (11.4). But with the advent of the male heir, Louis-Provence (for whom all the *Parlement* of Provence stood as godfathers), new worlds and freedom open for both correspondents. Provence had given Mme de Grignan what her mother's letters from Brittany could only approximate, the impossible gift of health and happiness. The letters' symbolic reunions pale before the excitement of the voyage to Provence and its reality of togetherness (9.27; 10.7; 10.11; 10.28; 12.2). Traveling back to Paris is the first step. The travel letter, again from Malicorne (12.13), looks now to the future, entirely focused by the excitement of receiving letters from Provence that take the imagination farther toward the coveted destination.

The mother's place in the Château of Grignan, she has been assured (6.28), is designated, and her presence welcomely awaited as a part of its new happiness. That knowledge sustains Mme de Sévigné through the long months in Paris of waiting for what seems the mirage of a "castle in Spain." With the new control and heroic self-testing evident by the time of the second anniversary of separation, there is also constriction. Increased tension of expectation makes life lived through letters seem to the letter-writer again a perpetual adieu. So it seems as Paris empties with mobilization for war, then seems filled with news of its deaths (6.20; 7.3.72), and as her aunt's death brings an adieu to another part of the Coulanges past (7.1.72). With the dream of Provence, the letter-writer bids adieu to her daughter, then goes to sleep in the room destined for the future with her, in the empty house in the rue de Trois-Pavillons (5.4.72).

As Mme de Sévigné prepared to return to Paris (12.9.71), the stay in Brittany envisioned with trepidation is at last given up with regret. There she had had new pleasures of letter-writing and new consolations through her art—"Provence has become my true country" (10.28.71). But the great discovery, as Duchêne notes apropos of "worry letters" and Mme de Grignan's lessening of their threats,[17] is that letters from the woods of Les Rochers need not be *about* anything. A walk in her own heart suffices to open the way to her daughter's, "that place where I long to be." The exuberance of the summer's games reflects the discovery and its increased momentum of confidence and hope. With them, a new frankness appears that six months earlier would have seemed unbearably transgressive speech.

This is the third time you have given birth in November; it will be September next, if you don't control it. Ask M. de Grignan for this reprieve in return for the pretty gift you have given him. . . . You have certainly suffered more than on a rack. Would he not despair, if he loves you, to cause your suffering such torture annually? Doesn't he fear losing you? I have nothing to add to these good arguments, except, by my faith, I shall not come to Provence if you are pregnant. (12.2.71)

Letters during Mme de Sévigné's fourteen-month stay in Provence, from and to her (Nos. 296-325), reveal nothing less than the happiness sought there. Mme de Grignan was again pregnant. But despite threats her mother had prepared herself for that potentially disappointing limitation of full freedom together. One discordant note comes from Mme de Lafayette, less indulgent than

Mme de Grignan with regular epistolary demands. Her warning was a lesson Mme de Sévigné had already learned. "You are in Provence, my pretty, your hours are free and your head freer. Your taste for writing everyone persists; mine for writing anyone has passed. If I had a lover who wanted my letters every morning, I would break with him. Don't measure friendship in writing" (6.30.73).

In the letters of first separation, no book had the power to give Mme de Sévigné the means of mastering the experience her mind confronts with courageous frankness and astonishing resourcefulness. Echoes of Corneille's heroism, of Molière's ridicule of unreason, of Pascal's central paradoxes, give letters forcefulness, intensity, and variety. But those echoes and the qualities they enhance resonate from the letter-writer's direct experience—of society and conversation, of old friendships and bonds with family and past, most of all in introspection and letter-writing that become inseparable acts. In all that experience La Rochefoucauld had a privileged place, his friendship and presence offering more than his book alone could have, during the period in which Mme de Sévigné reaches full mastery of her art. From the first days, as she pored anxiously over the map of her daughter's route south, La Rochefoucauld suggested a map for her mind. "M. de La Rochefoucauld says I confirm his idea of friendship's love (*amitié*) in all its effects and dependencies" (2.25.71). With discoveries in letter-writing of her love's unreason, the limits of her mind and letter-writing itself, the cruel ambiguities of love's search for self-satisfactions, Mme de Sévigné too explores La Rochefoucauld's anatomy of love, "in the soul a passion to dominate, for the mind a sympathy, and in the body a hidden and delicate desire for possession after many rituals" (68). Discoveries of the "uncharted regions on the map of self-love" she "civilizes," as she can, with her own style of perfect friendship.

The art and mind of the letters of first separation, which take the letter-writer beyond her consciousness of paradox and ambiguity, do not owe their power to the talent alone—much less the facility—of the solitary writer remaining a figure in the background. It depends essentially on Mme de Grignan's gift of life in responsive dialogue. Rescuing the writer from solitude, epistolary exchange gives substance and shape to Mme de Sévigné's letters, and sustains their celebration of perfect friendship. However intermittent and illusory, the letter-writer's transcendent reality in that perfection is a triumph of epistolary style over time, distance, and fragmentation of life.

CHAPTER 5

Illness and Grace (1673-1683)

I *Mother and Daughter*

THREE things Mme de Sévigné did not have to learn during
first separation from her daughter—to know herself, to understand her daughter, and how to write. All three she came to know
more fully, as communication and self-expression satisfied the
mother's needs. Personal truths of letter-writing, confirmed at
Grignan, are during the following decade memorialized at each new
separation: the second in 1675, third in 1677, a fourth climactic one
in 1679.

A special courtesy letter for the hospitality of tenderness at
Grignan summarizes personal truths as it commemorates the
"terrible day" of departure (10.5.73). Separation "gave me real
pain . . . my heart and imagination are filled with you. . . . It seems
I did not embrace you enough . . . tell you enough how contented I
am with your love for me. I am already consumed by curiosity and
hope for consolation only from your letters." A familiar poetry
(very like Lamartine's "sigh of the soul" in "Isolation")[1] crystallizes the letter—"I seek you always, and I find nothing, for I do not
find you." Tensions are reassumed. There is resignation to a future
that will repeat patterns of the past and also intensify them. "I shall
be all the more pitiable for having imprudently made the need to
see you a habit. . . . Adieu, my dear child, love me always: alas!
here we are with letters again." Finally there is repetition of the
sacrifice made at Livry: "I live only for you. God grant me the
grace to love Him as I do you."

Directness and sobriety underscore essential truths, as increasingly through the decade, with something like the "noble simplicity" admired in Mme de Grignan's style. "Do not celebrate
thoughts that oppress the heart," she advised again before second

separation. Its commemorative letter (5.27.75), another dense enumeration of her mother's personal truths, now includes efforts to be made shortly in Pentecostal ceremonies at Livry. "A little devotion" there could restore quietude, the love of God being "the only thing that must make you yield my heart" (5.29). But "occupied and filled" by her daughter, she is denied the sacrament and returns resignedly to the "house I cannot bear in your absence." Quietly, she prepared to go beyond it; opening her heart, as in an act of faith, she repeats: "It is to God alone that you must yield my heart" (6.5).

Against the unchanging personal truths of the style of perfect friendship, shared by the two correspondents, ordinary time seems to hold no challenges. But a decade's hard realities discover its vulnerabilities. Illness, weeks before Mme de Sévigné's fiftieth birthday, modifies letters organically. Middle age marks their complexion with lines of reflectiveness. And during the decade the two women are less separated than together, life in common brings the truths of presence—progressively tense strains threatening to reactivate those of the past (1670) and to solidify incompatibility as a definitive barrier to intimate exchanges. Each tantalizing approximation to the old dream of reunion in Paris makes its fulfillment seem to recede further into the domain of wishful thinking.

Pauline's birth in September 1674 gave the Marquise a new chance at the art of being a grandmother to which she had already warmed. It gave her also the excellent reasons of health and safety to urge a prolonged stay, extending the mother's pleasures to fifteen months (May 25, 1675). Annoyed by her mother's insistent planning (1.20.75), Mme de Grignan came to resent it as interference with her own life at Grignan. Her apologies for impatience are quickly silenced, in the interest of future life together. Letters' old truth in separation—"Could I be anything but happy with you?"—must not now have an affirmative answer, which would promote letters to more than the shadow of a fuller life together. Evidence to the contrary is conjured away, the letter-writer herself incriminating the partial truth of her first impulse to celebrate untroubled happiness. "Some persons have tried to make me believe that the fullness of my friendship was a burden for you, that its attentiveness to your desires, very naturally my own, assuredly caused you great weariness and distaste. . . . But I do not believe I was a burden to you" (6.7.75). If the two women must go their separate ways, and the mother "not know how to find my salvation," her letter clarifies, only an unjust providence is to be blamed. The same wishful thinking and explanation are not possible in 1677.

"Let us leave ourselves to providence," Mme de Sévigné wrote, happy with its gifts (10.15.77). News had reached her a fortnight earlier at Vichy that the house known as the Carnavalet had been secured, after protracted and uneasy delay. Gratitude for that part of the new "lease on life" felt at Vichy bursts with romanesque abandon: "I advance blindly, without knowing my destiny. What of it? It's a pleasure" (9.29.77). Letters leap and digress with the same freedom, of news and wit, and bristle with plans. In size and disposition,[2] the new house (for which the Grignans paid half the costly lease) renewed hopes, giving the dream of happiness the proper setting it had lacked in the less spacious house in the rue de Trois-Pavillons or, unexpectedly, in another leased in the rue Courteauvillain. There Mme de Grignan remained only briefly during a stay (December 22—end May 1677) before the third separation. The Carnavalet's "good air" was room for the Grignans' independence and privacy; a special "gray room" was set aside for Mme de Grignan, as were ample apartments for the Grignan family.

If Mme de Sévigné came with high hopes and special relief to the grand house that was her last Paris residence, it was the shortness of five months apart that especially seemed providence's gift after the impasse before the last separation. Burdens of maternal solicitude, with its implicit questioning of maturity and threats to her daughter's independence, had been compounded by guilt and worry and by poor health. Mme de Grignan's seriously altered beauty was noticed by others, who repeated the unwanted advice of 1675 on separation. With it this time came the authority of physicians and Grignan's to separate the two women living out the paradoxes of love's cruelty of Mme de Sévigné's first letters. Physicians reassured the family that Mme de Grignan's weak chest was not consumption; that travel would not unduly tax her; that competent physicians could also be found at Grignan, where the air was not "poisonous." Since overriding concern was for her daughter's well-being, Mme de Sévigné's reason wins out easily over fear of gossip, should health be restored away from its celebrated source, less easily over the greater fear of that precedent for the future of life together.

Promises are made, prudent reticence practiced, future plans continued more tactfully, all with one end in mind for letter-writing: "Let us show that we are reasonable enough to live together when providence wills" (6.27.77). But normal rhythms of correspondence are possible only through a tenacious and risky refusal to let go. Letters mercilessly replay events and agonize over blame (6.11; 6.14; 6.27; 6.30.77). As health did stabilize, the absurdity of the "cure" away from her is swallowed with thinly veiled self-degradation (7.19; 7.28; 7.30.77). Providence's harsh decrees must be accepted. But heart and mind find them as difficult as the oppressive thoughts of death each separation brings.

The Marquise was disposed to think appropriately on death. Sermons fortified her, as did contemplation on the Passion. She accepted death's presence in life (obituaries are from the first a part of her letters' life). Like her society,[3] she invests ritual preparations for death with special meaning, follows their protocol solemnly, and feels their formal celebration one of language's highest achievements. But there had been too many deaths in early life for her mind to dwell willingly on death or overcome panic the thought alone of Mme de Grignan's death raised in 1671.

In the lively summer of 1671, death still surprises her; hearing of her friend Bishop Lavardin's fatal stroke, she turns automatically to providence and stops dead: "Providence's decrees may please, but one must know how to profit from them. And poor Lenet, dead too; I'm vexed by it" (8.2). The "without time" of reflection on sudden death lingers as the kernel of the first significant meditation on death in the letters, in which self-demand again balances helplessness.

When the time comes, we shall certainly have faith beyond our means for our pains and travail. But time itself, which we squander and want the moment it slips from us, will be wanting, however much we would give everything for one of the days we lose with such indifference. That is the monologue in my woods. Christian morality is excellent for all ills, but I want it Christian. Otherwise it is hollow and meaningless. (9.20.71)

The Marquise practices with death. Disciplining repulsion by her aunt's slow death, she chronicles her own weakness in continuing counterpoint to Mme de La Trousse's edifying preparations (6.2;

6.6; 6.20; 6.24; 6.27.72). But the reflections on death Gide thought "turned out in a way that could not be equaled"[4] (3.16.72) are those filled with dread and resentment. Practice with providence brings only partial comfort at the loss of Retz (8.25.79), which like her thoughts on La Rochefoucauld's death (3.17.80) revives "the horror of separation"—from her daughter—there still as she confesses: "Everything suggesting an eternal separation pains the heart" (10.30.80). Death is never banalized in the letters.

Providence is another story. If a doctrine of providence is the letter-writer's *summa*,[5] the evolving shape of letters by 1677 gives witness to that "unique good." During dark days when old epistolary truths seem to her newly limited (reassurance of unchanged affection possible only with Mme de Grignan's return), Nicole seems "nonsense" (7.16.77) and skepticism the mind's only philosophy—"to speak of the future only as I feel my way" (7.30). But early experience of religion "venerable *and* lovable," intermittently reaffirmed, points another way to freedom. Powerless to control events most important to her, the letter-writer for the first time appeals to providence for both explanation and consolation for events in the lives of mother and daughter.[6] Feeling her way by letters, they change; "may it please God," "as providence wills," or a similar coordinate appears at every turning of her mind's discoveries of its limitations and her weaknesses. Powerless to command the heart's or even mind's full assent, the letter-writer's repetitions flog her, programmatically and almost literally, into "submission and use of reason, in which true Christianity consists," for her as surely as Pascal (Brunschvicg ed., no. 269).[7]

When the pattern of life together in 1677 repeated itself in 1679, forcing the fourth separation as the Carnavalet dream became a nightmare (November 1677-September 13, 1679), mother and letter-writer reach the lowest point in the correspondence. Under the weight of almost total breakdown in communication and the need for Grignan's presence in Paris (5.27.78), the old style of letter-writing shatters. The letter-writer's imagination flounders, deceiving her with hopes of reunion, she admits dispiritedly to Guitaut (9.12.79). Transparently wishful thinking glares through contradictions and strident insistence on old verities. Plans for the Carnavalet are left to Mme de Grignan "as mistress" and to God (9.13; 9.18), then taken up (10.4). Forgiveness and accusations come together in one letter (9.18), as uneasily as do often am-

biguous repetitions of old formulas with memories of the art that
once mastered distance—"You have accomplished perfectly the
Gospel's precept to leave all else for one's husband" (9.27)—or
mastered time: "I owe to your absence the pleasure of knowing my
life's time with its desolate stretches" (9.15). "I am abandoned to
my imagination" (10.11), she repeats in the unknowable and
uncontrollable gulf of time and solitude before the next reunion. In
it, the letter-writer is the more pitiable for her awareness, in the
letters of September and October, that "we exhaust language."

In response to the new needs, contingency plans are at hand—
Livry and providence, as the letter-writer rallies, "no less sensitive
but more resigned": "How can one lose sight of divine providence,
without hanging oneself five or six times a day. . . . Without Livry I
should have been ill" (To Guitaut, 12.6.79). More than a "little
devotion," or emulation of her daughter's "reason and courage,"
is now sought and found with a new beauty—and new understanding—desired in 1675, at Vichy, and in Brittany in 1680.

II   New Beauties (1675)

Passing the monastery of Port-Royal-in-the-Fields in 1674, Mme
de Sévigné felt (1.26) in that "fearsome valley of salvation" the
chilled awe she attaches to feelings of the "sublime." Her personal
symbol of the order of contemplative life, its ideal beauty seemed
elusive as ever. That sense of disproportion accompanies her on her
own way. It is a constant of mature letters, expressed in tones
varying from terse self-denigration to anguish, abandoned fatalism
to quiet resignation.

Her way led momentarily to a last conversation with a less
daunting incarnation of her symbol, d'Andilly, translator of such
spiritual classics as Augustine's *Confessions* (read in 1676) and the
Ladder of Divine Ascent by Saint John Climacus. His "direction"
and other Jansenist "brothers in truth" prompt new ponderings on
"the treasury of our heart's weaknesses," which seemed especially
written for her in Nicole's *Moral Essays* (still her "vinegar against
fainting"). In her favorites, "On the Means of Preserving Peace
among Men" (a *chef-d'œuvre* to Voltaire) and "On Submission to
God's Will," she found an ideal of reason that guards itself from a
spirit of contentiousness obscuring its highest good. So it had in her
early readings of Pascal's *Provincial Letters* a theology of grace she

was ready to hear in 1675 rereading. Above all, Nicole's analysis of the "hateful I" and "swollen heart"[8] haunts her letters. All Nicole, it almost came to seem, as it explained failures to ascend lastingly to contemplative order, seemingly so easy from the first step of moralizing among society's vanities. Assimilated as she wished, Nicole's writings offer one guide.[9] Others (Augustine, *Romans*, the Gospels, Pascal?) will be more compelling at decisive moments. Like d'Andilly, whose early advice to open her heart to God ultimately lights her way, Nicole's writings are a spark—not a burning bush.

The "solitary of Les Rochers" remained "at home" (unlike some other ladies who were friends of Port-Royal) within the bounds of her readings, occasional conversation and "disputation," most of all meditations nourished by the elective affinity her own inwardness·created. That "breathing freely" was the more difficult for cultivated habits of shunning sustained direction by a spiritual director, a regular confessor over the years, or a conventional pattern of retreats in convents other than that she fashioned herself "at home." The bedside devotional book of her society, Ribadeneira's *Florilegium of the Lives of the Saints*, found no place there. Nor did a cult of special saints or the rosary (Bossuet like Jansenists had warned against excessive devotion to Mary). On guard against the mind's enslavement by any "popular" devotion or by automatism, the Marquise purifies herself in 1675 as later: "I have left the Immaculate Conception of the Mother to keep myself entirely for the Son" (12.15.88). The chapel newly finished at Les Rochers in 1675 was at first given no other ornament than a painting of the Son.

The 1675 letters reveal an "enlightened mind" in a process of clarification and purification of "true doctrine" and "truly Christian" practice. That process remains a constant, like her sense of disproportion, whose expression is sharpened by it, and the complementary habit of personally reflective rather than speculative reading. Her own brand of common sense, repulsed by systems, persisted in finding stumbling blocks, in Descartes' body-soul dichotomy or Malebranche's occasionalism. But early in 1675 her mind is seriously in search of a system, whose beauty would be satisfaction for her of Descartes's desire for clear and certain knowledge of all that is useful for this life. She tries it out on Bussy (1.20.75).

All our desires do not advance providence's disposition a single moment. I believe that, my cousin; that is my philosophy. You in your way and I in mine follow the same route, aspiring to tranquility, you by reasoning and I by my submission. Your strength of mind and mine's docility lead us alike to scorn this world's goings-on. Truly they are little. We have little part in our destinies. All is in the hands of God.

Sympathy had already brought to more frequent correspondence with Bussy a new willingness to indulge him in his rhetoric of exile, tersely at first then more expansively and eloquently. But neither sympathy alone nor any desire to compose "publishable" fine letters restores the vitality of their exchanges, again the sharpener they had been for the young letter-writer. Docility with Bussy was in itself a good testing of the new philosophy, since he had accused her of fair-weather devotion (1.28.72). "It seems to me I no longer write well . . . your approbation would give me confidence," she bids (10.15.74) before the amplifications of her new philosophy seek that approbation. She practices with Guitaut too, less rhetorically, and with Judge Moulceau (in careful and slightly mannered banter of an old friendship seeking favors for the Grignans).[10] But it is with Bussy she can most profit, from a detached refinement of the less calm enterprise of letters to her daughter, for the heart's assent to the mind's newly firm directions. In those central letters to her daughter a new beauty of eloquence also appears, on death, continuing and amplifying earlier exercises in humility. Meditating on the death of her friend the great general Turenne, the letter-writer elaborates its details (7.31; 8.28.75), making them with the resounding knell of her repeated invocations a sublime exemplum of providence's decrees.

In letters from Brittany (Nos. 424-64), which could crown the year's purifications, the "holiday" metaphor does yield some place to one of "retreat." As though in keeping with conventions of devotional writing, meditation in its natural setting seems at the point of becoming contemplation *through* it. But unable or unwilling to sacrifice her woods' old privileges as settings for the correspondents' walks through the mother's heart, "retreat" becomes flight. A new walkway, "The Solitary," is "made expressly for right meditation." But in it, all seems still at Mme de Grignan's "direction." "*You* would profit from it, *and I* don't use it too badly. . . . I think of you every moment. . . ." "God's will must be regarded fixedly," she admits, "in order to envisage without despair everything I see and surely shall not speak of to you" (9.29, my emphasis). "Retreat" is made to her tower-room with its books, which becomes a second privileged center of letter-writing, alternating and in tension with the first. Their two perspectives, of the loved one's "direction" and God's will, are maintained in separate clarity and purity by the letter-writer, until illness in 1676 distorts her vision.

The dream for Les Rochers is of a new quietude (after trying financial worries with added anxieties caused by new examples of the King's deafness to petitions). "I shall love to know the docility of my mind and to follow the examples of your courage and reason. . . . I shall remember your sermons" (9.6). But symptomatically, mention of letter-writing—the reality of "my poor life" to come—breaks the dream, sending the letter-writer back to the refuge of past epistolary beauties. "I shall read, walk, write, and receive your letters. Alas! life passes too quickly and exhausts itself everywhere." Some calm is found. "You would like my sobriety and the exercises I do, and seven hours abed like a Carmelite. This harsh life pleases me" (10.13.75). But the mind's quietude does not follow. Neither reading, more serious but still unfocused, nor the love coveted with docility tempers the harshness of the venerable truth of providence's justice in all things or opens the way to other exercises that will.

As she writes of new beauty (9.9), the distance from Mme de Sévigné's old banter on her heart's ice is great: "Nothing is so good, my dear daughter, as a good and beautiful soul. It is visible in all things as through a heart of crystal. . . . One must be that, one must be, if one desires to appear so." The distance is infinitely greater, Pascal might say, separating the letter-writer from the appearance of serenity that will come, significantly in a meditation on death (of mother and daughter). "If only I had a heart of crystal in which you could see the pain. . . . God, to whom our hearts are open, knows its ardor perfectly" (1.10.80). Both providence and her "little part" in her destiny chart her course.

III *Vichy*

Letters from excursions to Vichy (Nos. 509-23, 600-16) are Mme de Sévigné's last series of brilliant letters. Life itself there was not brilliant. The fashionable spa, much like Bath for eighteenth-

century English society, was Bourbon-l'Archambault. Its "cere-
monial" the Marquise chronicled on a visit with the Duchesse de
Chaulnes in 1687 (Nos. 978-84), without much interest or the
sparks that make Vichy letters more than a "piquant travel
album."[11]

Vivid in descriptions, sharp portraits, pure laughter, the Vichy
letters convey a continuing illusion of keen openness and delight in
new experience. Within hailing distance of *L'Astrée* country, there
are a few nostalgic memories of the novel. But the letters are as free
from literary modeling as those from Brittany that had refreshed
the familiar with their own scenes of provincial society, rustic life,
and solitary meditation. If curiosity seems limited to rediscovery of
the pleasures of those letters, for good reasons, it outdistances in
freedom and reflectiveness the *Voyage* (1663) of the libertine
"philosophers" Chapelle and Bachaumont, which became a
literary model for others.

Good reason beyond economy made the Marquise depart from
Mme de Montespan's recent route to Bourbon, reported (5.16.76)
as all the "Beautiful Lady" 's doings are, and shun its society for
Vichy's waters, touted for migraines and lethargy, faulty memory
and failing eyesight, warming the stomach, cleansing liver and
spleen, easing colics and rheumatism. The development of rheumatism, begun with a twisted neck (1.15.76), compelled her to seek a
"straight and narrow" cure. It had immobilized the right side, then
both legs and arms, hands and feet. Pain and high fever, abated
over three weeks but "mixing my realities," left an impatient and
depressed convalescent at Les Rochers, unable to leave before
March and humiliated in others' care despite Charles's attentiveness. The point passed for old riddles (2.3), whose wit postponed
naming the cause but not the reality of painfully restricted movement. Dictating did not bring old consolations of letter-writing,
either the muscular pleasure of her rapid writing or the intimacy,
now necessarily limited. As long as illness lingered, even as writing
became possible, the threat remained of chronic impairment of
epistolarity (3.8; 3.24).

Attuned to the medical world, and annoyed by its failures in
three generations (her grandson had recently been prescribed
"abominable" treatment to straighten his back), the Marquise may
have been especially receptive to reports marveling on "the grace of
God and the effects of the waters." If some idea of God's punish-

ment, in her writing hand of that part she felt most sinning against Him, lurked in her mind, so too may have a hope of His miracle through the waters. Preoccupied letters since March suggest she may have been no more certain about the waters themselves, since physicians warned: "Tranquility of the passions is the first requirement for the body's proper function while taking the waters."[12] Her own illness, Mme de Grignan's convalescence after premature birth, Charles's departure with the army (whose movements remain news in her letters), left little place for tranquility.

Her coach and six covered the route in eight days of good speed. New sights, light reading, easy conversation with an old friend needed as companion, delight the letter-writer and liberated shut-in, glad to report "fine views that surprise us every moment" (5.16.76). Unable to be the exotic bird of passage she enjoyed being, the Marquise who felt herself more "poor wet hen" (3.15) avoided friends and family. But an exception was made at Moulins. Usually uneasy with greeting in Visitation convents as a "living relic" (of the founder), this time it was a welcome bidding to brief retreat.

"Keenly pious emotion" may have been felt,[13] but it is muted in the calm letter from the room where Mother de Chantal had died (5.17). Filled with plans and news, it seems a typical travel letter, secular as La Fontaine's on the empty Château of Richelieu or hers on Vaux with its fountains silent (7.1.76). But pity and envy for a religious vocation, briefly at its center, do echo the humbling Livry experience. Filling another room with thoughts of her daughter, seeking peace that way in this room, the letter-writer may again have felt how different Mother de Chantal's way had been. That feeling had recently come to her at Bourbilly. Returning to the empty château, where her grandparents' marriage had flourished and its loss became Mother de Chantal's bridge to God, she wrote: "Better than I have lived here" (10.16.73). In Burgundy she preferred staying with the living, the Guitauts at Epoisses; so does she on return from Vichy in June. When no miracle has happened at Vichy and Mme de Grignan's much planned winter in Paris is canceled, she stays with Mme Foucquet.

Leaving Moulins, Mme de Sévigné is the more alone for determination to keep some secrets, some of herself apart from letter-writing, for her convalescent daughter's sake but also for her own. When friends drive out to welcome her to Vichy (5.19.76), the unexpected caress of the familiar takes the chill from the unknown she dreaded. Vichy too had its caresses but only in repayment for some yet unknown slaps to the Marquise's dignity.

Life in the White Horse Inn on the Pont-Neuf is made to seem a camping out, refreshingly simple and improvisational. "How nasty the waters are," the Marquise shudders, swallowing them (six times more than now recommended) as she does potential boredom (5.19-21). Sparing herself prescribed morning purges, she seeks hers in the countryside that seems a burst of song and dancing. "The beauty of the walks . . . alone will restore my health" (5.24). Exhilarated by rustic dancers' bourrées, she provides them a violin and drum "for four sous every evening in these meadows." Taking her upbeat from the duple time of their flute, her letters flush with pleasure in the open air (5.26; 6.8), significantly free from the burden of memories of Mlle de Sévigné dancing. "The peasant men and women have a keener ear than you, lightness, form, I'm mad for it." As irresistibly, the letter-writer organizes new "bad copies of better originals," her own in the wet hen's progress, others with malicious type-casting.

The "perfect beauty" the Duchesse de Brissac (estranged from her husband but always perfect to her half-brother Saint-Simon) casts herself. Posing in decorous illness but quickly bored, she plays the comedy of coquetry at high speed for a passing priest (5.26), raising the letter-writer's eyebrows. The comedy of two older women is grotesque and savage. "Mme de La Baroire stammers with apoplexy and is pitiful. But when one sees her ugly and no longer young . . . and reflects that after twenty-two years of widowhood she fell for M. de La Baroire, attached publicly to another, gave him everything though he slept with her only a quarter of an hour, that he threw her out (what a long development!), but thinking of it all one has the urge to spit in her face" (6.4). The parenthetical self-mockery no more softens the slap than friendship does another dealt Mme de Péquigny, the Duc de Chaulnes's mother—"the Cumean sybil, decked out girlishly." "She believes she can cure herself of the obvious embarrassment of being seventy-six. For that Vichy would need the fountain of youth." "A madhouse," she complains as much to herself as for her daughter's amusement, when that "strange machine" apes her to be as well and horrifies rather than touches her. The not so humble wet hen continues her therapies at the spring—and in letter-writing—grateful for even a blemished image of "Mother Beauty."

Stripped of clothing and identity, the Marquise has a further demonstration of mortality that illness had already given her (4.10.76). As she descends into the bath (5.28), humiliation and hypersensitivity to the scalding water project painful vulnerability that escapes the humorously set scene. "Purgatory," she shudders, indeed like its primitive depiction in churches she visited.

If "women's hell is old age," as La Rochefoucauld reminded Ninon, Mme de Sévigné has of that special purgatory of middle age at Vichy a vision whose macabre comedy resembles the sanitarium of Mann's *The Magic Mountain*. Nightmares of incapacitated old age and its automatisms loom before her in the stultifying schedules and tawdry comedy of the "curists," their absurd quest for youth reflecting her own. At one moment she may delight in a rose brought to full bloom in the hot springwater. But for another, after reading Mme de Grignan's reference to lice, she superimposes onto her innocent news a horrifyingly surreal self-image (5.24.76).

The brightness of the Vichy letters goes beyond the games of health of letters from Brittany, as though in part intermittent fever, or giddiness from the surfeit of water. Nightmares go beyond vanity (Nicole's "On Self-Love" was taken to heart, 1.12; 4.22.76). Being a burden and an embarrassment to her daughter is the nightmare. With it the heart falters that controlled letter-writing and time by scenes of mother and daughter beautiful in intimacy, now frozen in the past like health itself. For the "enemy of false news," that kind of timelessness was no temptation.

Struggling to exorcise nightmares, the letter-writer pinches herself to life. Letters of the second stay, when there is no bath, exorcise the first (and separation). Before it with Bussy, on an excursion turned into a ribald game-letter with Guitaut (8.29.77), during leisurely return to Paris, the bloom of health is patted into the letter-writer's reflection. At Crosne, her account of visiting the forge triumphs over the descent into the bath. In the hot darkness near the sweating men at work, the emotion vivifying the letter's fantasy of a "veritable hell" is a gladly felt and shared eroticism (10.1.77). "I may still be your *bellissima madre*," she had wished touchingly (5.28.76), then affirmed (6.21.76), and finally confirms by her own letters and Coulanges' new compliments to an "incomparable Mother Beauty" (10.7.77).

The "new lease on life" (5.28.76) given by Vichy is a new compromise with time and aging, a new acceptance of herself, possible by the gift of health that will allow the Marquise to remain herself and grow old gracefully. While waiting for the grace that may come, and that of her daughter's gaze, she pursues letter-writing appropriately. She watches for flaccidness, which as in early 1676 betrays an involuntary relaxation exacted by aging. But she watches also over another, on which she has no illusions. "You ask me whether I am devout, *ma bonne*; alas, no, to my chagrin. But I am a bit more detached from what is called the world. Old age and a little illness give time for great reflections" (6.8.76). Befitting her age and notion of "proper use of illness," the letter-writer gives herself more to devotion. If nothing more, doing so is prudent—"following the ordinary actions of good little human prudence, the way, I believe, of reaching the order of providence" (10.7.76).

IV   *Brittany and Providence*

There is no "conversion," dramatically cutting away worldliness, in Mme de Sévigné's letters, no Pascalian "night of fire" memorialized by them. But there is apparent in the correspondence of 1680 (Nos. 722-830) a kind of letter whose contours of thought and style are those of a "devotional letter," transforming the letters of 1671-72, by what has seemed a "paroxysm of Jansenist sermonizing."[14]

If the quality of the Marquise's spiritual progress in 1680 may seem to us ambiguous and questionable[15] (only great saints perhaps find the full clarity of that expression), there is no doubt that the letter-writer feels a spiritual progress by the end of the year, which culminates efforts since 1671 to accommodate and center animating devotion within her life. It is expressed to Mme de Grignan (9.11; 9.18; 10.9.80) with conviction that reflects also in letters to Bussy (from 4.3.81). But it is recorded also by the changing shape and function of letters themselves, as meditation on devotion, more actively pursued and sustained in central monologues, strives to come to terms with the *cogito* of spirituality perceived at Livry (3.24-26.71). Felt with growing urgency in 1673 (10.5; 12.4) and 1675 (5.29; 6.5; 6.26), it is given striking relief in 1680 by the repeated phrase "an enlightened mind, a heart of ice." That stark self-image is at the center of personal meditations which are not simply sermonizing or the transcript of spiritual exercises.

The repeated Livry experience of contradiction, through a long series of rooms in convents and at home after first separation from her daughter, closed the letter-writer still in 1680 into a *cachot* (dungeon) with a consciousness of enclosure as intense as Pascal's memorable fragments on disproportion (Br. 200, 205, 208, 211).[16] "Ah, my God, truly we are Tantaluses. We have water just at our lips but cannot drink; a heart of ice, an enlightened mind. I don't need the quarrel of the Jansenists and Jesuits to see that. What I feel in myself suffices" (5.1.80).

More than the need to renounce the role of providence's scenario-writer was thus felt in letters of April and May. To transcend the pattern of broken promises of reunion, and dependence on correspondence felt by fourth separation as inextirpable weakness, letter-writing itself must participate in spiritual exercises. To make letters do that, more than metaphorically, is Mme de Sévigné's last and most difficult self-demand. The logic of meditations demanded essential modifications; if not total sacrifice, of what seemed already in 1677 on the way to being an "old style" but remained nonetheless the cherished permanence of the past. "The pains which are attached to the tenderness I have for you, offered to God, are the penitence of an attachment that should only be for him" (4.3.80). Pains and penitence are stressed in 1680, as Duchêne indicates,[17] and among them is the painful dying to the epistolary past.

"By the machine," Pascal advised, "write the letter, about removing obstacles, that is the argument of the machine, how to prepare it and how to use reason for the search" (Br. 246, 248).[18] Write the letter Mme de Sévigné does in 1680, over and over again, grappling the "heart of ice" on her new voyage to Brittany through the prior problem of "submission *and* use" of reason, which can and does turn the intimations of 1675 into an efficacious program in 1680.

Preparing herself differently for this voyage and stay, the letter-writer breaks the ritual pattern of adieu letters, "inclining the machine" with a gesture of submission (5.6.80).

I need the creator of the world to understand everything that happens. If I must blame Him, I no longer blame anyone else. I am submissive, but not without pain and sadness. My heart is pierced. But even those pains I suffer as being in the order of providence. There has to be a Mme de

Sévigné, who loves her daughter more than any other mother loves, who has often to be far from her, who has to suffer her sharpest pains from her dear daughter.

A further step beyond this incomplete gesture is taken with Guitaut (5.18). Priming the pump, in an ostensibly spontaneous outburst of central monologue on providence, the Marquise sets one of her characteristic balance-sheets, counting prior efforts of her mind at nought in proportion to that "unique good." "But what can one do with an enlightened mind and a heart of ice? There's the misery, for which I know no remedy save asking God for the degree of heat so needed. But it is God who causes us to ask properly." What the letter-writer does, as "providence stabilizes my thoughts and gives me some peace," is to forget the momentary flirtation with revolt and continue priming the pump, with her daughter (5.21), in a sermon for both of them (beginning "I don't understand the great mystery you make of God's providence . . ."). Asserting her own views, rather than reflecting Mme de Grignan's, she takes the "discourse of the machine" to its breaking point of an explanation of the inexplicable, an equilibrium of the polarities of free will and predestination.

Having opened to God her heart's ardor (1.10.80) and desire, for the greater freedom "of the children of God" discussed with Corbinelli before departure (5.1), the Marquise seems as determined to make good use of traveling as she had of illness. There is now no question of whiling away the time with the "breviary of Corneille." But neither is there the possibility of turning the "beautiful freedom" of her Loire into the litany of her uncle's *Ave*'s (5.12). Bent on difference (which might come through humility), the travel letters leave her frustrated at Nantes, in a cloud of familiar and contentious language (as though it had used itself). Yearning for Les Rochers, where "breathing freely" will be possible, her failure encloses her once more. The letter of May 25, a "magnificent self-analysis,"[19] should culminate earlier introspective letters inspired by the divided heart. But no spiritual transcendence of temporal enclosure takes place. There is no transmutation, through the voluntary servitude she muses on from Nicole's "On Submission to the Will of God," into the place of hope and peace Pascal's "happy dungeon" becomes.[20]

A different experience is memorialized in the "torrent I cannot stop" of July 14. One of the many "sermonizing" letters, its synthesis elevates it to a special place. Meditation begins with Saint Augustine, whose treatises *On the Predestination of the Saints* and *On Perseverance* the letter-writer had been reading (6.26; first, 10.21.76) with the feeling of finding both the pure doctrine of the Church on grace and all the errors of her "poor heart." "It is better to trust to divine promise than to one's will" is the rubric of the section[21] in which she found a truth so self-evident as to withstand any controversy and familiar counsel—since you do not know whether you are among the elect, strive as though you were. By the end of June, there had already been a turning point, and a turning away from reading, to a new quality of submission and humility. "Truly, I do not understand and am fully disposed to recognize the mystery of free will. Since it cannot put our salvation into our hands, and dependence on God must always be, I don't seek to be enlightened any further and wish to remain, *if I can*, in humility and dependence" (6.21, my emphasis). "If I can" is the habitual protasis of epistolary devotions that bring satisfactions and reassurance.

Beginning on July 14 as though a gloss on *Romans* (IX:18, 20-21), and characteristically seeking companion texts from the gospel (*John* X:14; XV:16), the meditation emerging from the cluttered "torrent" is an Augustinianism as purified as Pascal sought to make it through his writings on grace. With it, an unflinchingly calm personal profession of faith ends the letter as it begins, with submission to "whatever is, is right" and with the Son.

God disposes of His creatures like the potter. He chooses, He rejects His creatures. They need not labor at compliments to assure His justice, for there is no other than His will. . . . He rejects because of original sin, the foundation of everything, and is merciful to the small number He saves through His Son.

To prolong the moment, the "vinegar" of Nicole's "On Perseverance" is at the ready. But the letter-writer goes on herself also with the program present to her mind earlier in the year. At this moment when original sin is the foundation of all, La Rochefoucauld is tellingly brought into the company of vain users of language. His model of analysis, of the mind's dependencies, is as much of her past as the letter-writing she now pictures in resigned lucidity—"we exhaust language." At the moment of the convergence of her guides—with her own way—there seems to be the heart's assent to the mind's new mode of explanation.

"Whatever is, is right" may have come more easily to the Marquise than to Voltaire, but for the woman and letter-writer who judged by the heart's capacity to love it came no more naturally. To overcome a lifetime's revulsion by moral and aesthetic automatism, and exaltations by freedom, demanded a rigorous redirection of "habitual thought," whose conditioning powers the letter-writer of 1671-72 knew so well. In the letters from 1675 through 1680, the rallying cry "providence" must displace "ridiculous" in frequency, as it supplants "wit" in the mind's new explanations. As doctrinaire recourse to providence strives harshly after its ends, the letter-writer opens herself to charges of fatalism, close to the kind of superstition she deplored (like Bayle she could not countenance [1.2.81] belief in occult powers of comets). Rigidity remains in 1680, on the necessity of contrition for participation in the sacrament of communion, for example, or in doctrinal rigor on the damnation of infants dying without baptism that exceeds her daughter's (6.21; 7.17). Harshness on Breton peasants, whose acts threatened order in 1675, exceeds anyone's, if one were to believe readers scandalized by her apparent cruelty.[22] That cruelty is strikingly in contradiction with her compassionate view of "souls straighter than lines, loving virtue as naturally as horses trot" (6.21.80) and resignation to a destitution that will not allow their payment of what she is due (6.9.80).

Compassion and resignation lead the letter-writer out of contradictions, as she begins (by the end of 1680) to wean herself and letters from rigid dependence on and mechanical invocations of providence. As surprising as any contradiction is one that becomes evident as letters are described as "torrents" or, in a new sense of the old description of fine disorder, as *fagots* (bundles of sticks); the letter-writer yearns to be free of memory or "this damnable wit"; "desolate stretches" of prosy flatness and fatigue with letter-writing are not hidden. Writing badly—or at least plainly—in penance for past epistolary vanities? The unthinkable for the letter-writer at the beginning of the decade is a reality at its end.

Letter-writing, as spiritual exercises, continues and expands Vichy's new lease on life. If from Vichy there came resignation to loss of the perfection of the Marquise's youthful prose portraits, through 1680 she resigns herself to a spiritual life precluding a sublime incarnation of contemplative life. She will be free of the troubling obsession with Mother de Chantal's way, as she had become of the phantoms of old age. "My father used to say that he loved God when he was well off; it seems to me I am his daughter" (9.11.80), the letter-writer can confess calmly, with her own "provisions" made for "the little time we have left." Her "little part we have in our destinies" will continue in the consolidated serenity achieved through the year's multiple resignations, which in quieter "new devotional letters" infuse the spirit of central monologues into them without the mechanical invocations of providence. The letter of June 21, among many, gives witness to that serenity, which eases the tension of "I am not a saint, there's the misfortune" (3.7.85) and also pitches the old romanesque abandon to the destinies of mother and daughter ("I advance blindly . . .") in the different key of "The roads are beautiful. God will lead us, I hope" (10.20.80). And in this new register of prayer, the letter-writer is master of her time—"The little time we have left will soon be past, my *bonne*, may it please God to give you health" (9.25.80).

The permanent marks left on letters by the struggle for spiritual autonomy and its satisfactions are a naturalization of them. When strength of mind or exaltations by old beauties are felt, the letter-writer henceforth moves toward humility; toward penitence and prayer, when there seems only weakness. It is Pascal's resolution of the dialectic of "grandeur and wretchedness,"[23] there for her with acceptance of Augustine's last word—beyond which there is only the mystery of God's will—strive as though you were. The condition of that striving, and its tone in later letters that purify the style of perfect friendship without renouncing it, is recorded in the series of letters framed by an assertive personal celebration of providence's beneficence. Freeing herself of her daughter's "direction," the letter-writer first insists (5.6.80) on the unique good of a love—"divine providence that I adore" (5.31-80)—which is returned by "particular graces" (9.11; 9.18; 9.29.80). Failure to question that questionable grace has seemed embarrassing. But in response to her daughter's reluctance to see those "signs" in the Grignans' recent good fortunes, the letter-writer's insistence justifies "special love" and finds the new beauty she desired of a transparent illustration of its indwelling.

CHAPTER 6

Last Accounts (1684-1696)

I Carnavalet

TO the end of her life, Mme de Sévigné's letters continue their reorderings of her time, day by day, which gave her letters their first distinctive textures. However enthusiastically they are sought by others who applaud their descriptions or wish their news, letters remain private, written always with her correspondents, herself, and her messages in view, never future readers of a published correspondence. And among her correspondents, Mme de Grignan remains in the first place. "You are too *plaisante* [droll] to have read in public my letter on the chevaliers; you make of me and my letters all that you wish them to be" (1.19.89). Letters of the last years contain few surprises. Even the most often admired among them suggest amplifications and refinements of the epistolary past.

The "relation"-letter describing Racine's *Esther* performed at Saint-Cyr (2.21.89), culminating in a brief exchange with the King envied by other courtiers, seems a rewriting of the letter recounting Séguier's funeral. Mme de Grignan's absence again provides the background, against which the same sensual evocation of an unfolding and enveloping spectacle (music and drama, gossip and news) are communicated. But the concerted efforts for "communion," at every point in the earlier letter, as well as its sharpness of irreverent wit and pain of separation, are significantly gone. The equally well-known letter to Coulanges on Louvois's death (7.26.91), in which Sainte-Beuve heard a "sublimity" like Bossuet's in his sermons,[1] is also enriched by the epistolary past. Expansive dramatization of the setting of Louvois's daily ministerial business, portentously preparing death's entrance, is a chastened art of display of the "Coulanges letter" on Mademoiselle's marriage, combined with the concentrated exemplum of the letters on Turenne's death ("Read Saint Augustine!"). Both amplification and consolidation by the moralist, the letter is shaped by its writer's pleasure in the expressive resources at her command. "Reading teaches one to write . . . and it's a fine thing to be able to write what one thinks," the letter-writer reflects, especially if the writing is like the speaking, "then you have it all" (7.17.89).

But as the letter-writer realized at Vichy and showed in 1680, "there comes a time when style must change . . . the mind narrows in one way and opens in another" (6.5.89). In contrast to the "pride, confidence, and beauty" of youth recalled in this letter, and the "springtime of humor" it recalls in her earlier letters, those from 1684 on seem autumnal. The "sublime" is still there as the old admirer of Corneille is "raised up, transported, in ecstasy" in her own fashion, but it is the less heady utility of his plays as a school for virtue that is now extolled. Molière very often still lends the letter-writer his angle of vision. But comic scenes, like extended "relations" in general or malicious wit, are rare. "Sermonizing," too, all but disappears. Pleasures of discovery, of changing views in travel or changing seasons, continue with and for delight, as do news of public events and private happenings or the novelties of recently heard anecdotes and new books. But they have neither the nervous restlessness of earlier letters nor their suggestiveness of the joys of a child's world. Sociability and movement in itself, on a scale that has ruined many writers, still spin off and energize letter-writing. What has gone from it all is extravagance, from the expression of love as well, leveled also in the newly unifying tone of prudent moderation.

By 1689-90, the predominant impression letters since 1684 create is one of business as usual. As the letter-writer repeatedly describes them, letters are the record of life "day by day," and they often seem the "tittle-tattle" and "endless repetitions" found mediocre by Lady Mary Montagu.[2] But the last transformation of epistolary art is not simply a loss of art, relaxation into a plain chronicle that sometimes seemed to the Marquise the most prudent letter-writing. Relaxation is a calculated effect of the writer's last manner, subtle and patient modulation of the past pleasures and victories of letter-writing, in response to new circumstances that had given it new structuring patterns and gave new significance to letters whose business it became to live day by day.

Financial and legal difficulties, diminished resources that include limited leverage at Court, deaths, are the realities in part already familiar in 1684, whose tensions now shape letters written against the backdrop of the diminishing expectations of advancing age. The restricted and reluctant place given to financial bulletins in earlier letters, in 1671-72 and even through 1680, is no longer possible. Responsibilities, honor, concern allow few letters to neglect business. It more often occupies the body of letters that "rounds off the dispatch." What is most notably and critically rounded off among the Marquise's reckonings is a final accounting to her son.

Charles's plunge at last into matrimony (February 8, 1684), with Jeanne-Marguerite de Bréhant de Mauron, twenty-four-year-old daughter of a well-to-do counselor in the *Parlement* at Rennes, followed months of financial reorganization that essentially altered the conditions of Mme de Sévigné's life. In her accounting for Henri de Sévigné's estate to her children in 1683, the mother was generous, exceptionally for her time and in her sacrifices. To give Charles his rightful share involved more than transfer of lands. He received Les Rochers and the full Sévigné domain in Brittany. But his debts were also paid, including the substantial amount owed to his mother (56,187 livres in June 1683) and on his commission to others. He acquired thereby the quite acceptable annual income of 11,000 livres. Keeping only her dower revenue from the Buron estate, his mother sold and transferred securities and juggled loan payments. The sum of 175,000 livres given in all to Charles matched what had been settled on Mme de Grignan in 1669, except for the value of Charles's share diminished by intervening devaluations (a good sum that troubled his prospective father-in-law).

Treating her two children equally, Mme de Sévigné reduced her own annual income by 4,000 livres for her son in 1683 as she had reduced it in 1669 by 3,000 for her daughter. What remained was a less than comfortable annual 7,700 livres.[3] To satisfy the finicky Bréhant, who unjustly thought delays implied Mme de Grignan's hedging for greater personal advantage (Charles reveals, No. 876, January 1684), his sister, too, made sacrifices to assure the good marriage the Sévignés all considered a windfall. In return for what was promised in 1669, she accepted the estate of Bourbilly, in place of a settlement in cash the Grignans sorely needed. In agreement with Bréhant's wishes, she also renounced future claims on her mother's estate.[4] As Duchêne has demonstrated, after a long history of allegations to the contrary, it was Charles rather than his sister who had things his way and to his advantage in 1683.

Tensions that grew between mother and son, explaining her failure to leave the Carnavalet for his wedding, resulted neither from withheld maternal love nor reluctance over family sacrifices made in 1683. They came from Bréhant, whose rudeness was felt an insult to the family and long rankled (for example, 12.8.83; 3.1.84). Charles in his impatience had not dissociated himself properly from the injustice and suffered a share of his mother's disgruntlement. Much like his father, but with his mother's sensibilities, Charles had winning ways with her. He was often forgiven after the proper severity. Never long out of his mother's graces, he was by the end of 1684 lastingly restored to them.

Charles's place in his mother's letters, as at Les Rochers during her illness in 1676 and in later gloom, is greater than his diverting treasury of follies in half-hearted courtships, long hours of reading aloud, and sharp-minded conversation. News of the war becomes in large measure part of letters because it is news of Charles. His movements are followed; distinctions in action at Seneffe and Bouchain (1674, 1676), Valenciennes and Mons (1677-78) are reported with satisfaction.[5] His returns to Les Rochers, delayed as he followed the whims of the road, are invariably evoked as delightful surprises. When the casualty and surprise brought home in summer 1680 was venereal disease, the noble lady touches off the mother's indignation worthy of any satirist: "There are women . . ." (8.28.80). Charles's misery brought sympathy and efforts to cheer him as he worsened and suffered grueling treatment (that most probably left him impotent). No doubt there were sermons, but they are conspicuously absent from letters. Sermons on indecisiveness, casualness with money, and limited ambition were also forthcoming, judging from exasperations expressed to Mme de Grignan. Those confidences sound less like insidious belittling than echoes of—or rehearsals for—what was quite properly said directly to "little brother," with his "gift for making the best things go bad" (7.17.80). Love expressed itself differently for a son, conventionally, and especially one felt too like his father and too dependent upon his mother. But it is expressed no less naturally.

Recounting a brief business visit to Buron, Mme de Sévigné's letter is weighed by depression over the dilapidation of the place.

She turns elegiac with memories of its forests, recently cut and sold by Charles for a good sum, then snaps that "he hadn't a sou from it a month hence" (5.27.80). "His hands are like a melting pot," she complains, and it is unlikely she resisted repeating the remark to him. Failure to receive preferment for a second-lieutenancy, after the wounds and distinctions of ten years in the army and at Court, depressed mother and son. Investment in his career only began with the commission for which she borrowed in 1669. It had to be maintained, with at least five loans by 1678, and in 1679 created difficulties illustrating the maneuverings that become the rule in Mme de Sévigné's life after 1683. In March, 15,000 livres were borrowed from d'Harouys, the cousin who had lent generously to the family in 1669. The loan was needed to pay off the balance (July) on the commission. And to repay d'Harouys (November), money was borrowed again from another generous past creditor, d'Ormesson.[6]

Justifiably vexed by the prospect of the commission's sale (effected 1.22.83) at a loss she ultimately had to assume (2.14; 3.6; 3.26.80), annoyance over Charles's flagging ambition and growing attraction to the life of a country squire is mixed with regret. But that regret, expressed more than once to Mme de Grignan, is for his sacrifice of a career. To sell the commission meant to resign from the King's service, consequently to withdraw from Court and renounce favor that came only there. If the Marquise herself by 1680 visited Court only about once a year, it was not by her choice. "I would have liked that country" (5.31.80), she confesses, and she often regrets that family interests are not more represented there. At Court Charles looked fine, Mme de Lafayette had reported with his need for money (2.9; 27.73); and he was after all, his mother knew, no fool. Letters are once again a place of resignation. She was sympathetic certainly to a desire for freedom, especially from service unjustly rewarded: "I feel keenly the attractiveness of his place, but I change with him; I too want freedom" (3.6.80). The change is for the best, despite lost money, if "he is happy where he now is. His unhappiness makes me more unhappy than the rest. Enough said about the rest" (7.3.80).

The habitual frankness between mother and son created some difficult days, but it also brought an untroubled life together after 1684. And Charles's frequently inserted notes to his "beautiful little sister," indistinguishable from his mother's letters except for the burdens of a better education, betray no resentment of the emotional favors lavished on his sister. When in 1683 there were tensions with both, Charles cleared the air in his mother's fashion with a disarmingly frank letter, whose last paragraph suggests his grandfather's Rabutin histrionics (No. 876).[7]

My heart contracts to hear you refer to your room at Les Rochers as your late room. Have you renounced it? Would you break with your son after doing so much for him? Deprive him of you as though in punishment? My marriage could not compensate for such unhappiness. . . . Write to me, I beg you, for truly my heart is so heavy I could not keep from weeping if I were alone. Adieu, don't renounce your son who adores you and wishes your every happiness as truly and ardently as his own salvation.

As revealing of the new situation as anything is the first sentence. The bitterest sacrifice for the Marquise may well have been the "sweet freedom" of Les Rochers. All sentimentality aside, it symbolized a special security, paying its way as it did more dependably than inherited securities (largely liquidated at a loss in 1681 after royal edict forced sales at market value). If a room was assured for her there, it was no longer the mistress's. There was another Mme de Sévigné. Although Charles constituted Les Rochers his mother's residence by legal action (and did assume some of her debts), a sense of dispossession remains when business demanded her first visit after the marriage. She found "no reason to feel that there is another mistress than I in this house, where I take charge of nothing but am served by little invisible orders" (9.27.84), but she nonetheless felt: "What I possess is no longer mine" (11.15.84).

The consequences of Mme de Sévigné's generosity in 1683, including her word to leave her estate free of new debts that precluded new borrowings not otherwise balanced, gave literal truth also to the resolution in the same letter. "One must end with the same honor and probity professed throughout a lifetime." Her letters henceforth are, as much as anything, the material record of that vow of genteel poverty, only beginning with the sacrifice of her own carriage. "I won't be ashamed," she wrote, "my children have fine ones, and I did too once: times change" (8.15.85). "I know the pleasures of decorating a room. . . . I have preferred paying debts, conscience obliging me, I believe, to do so, and justice to have no new ones'' (6.13.85).

The death of the *Bien Bon* (''Good Indeed''), as Christophe de Coulanges is affectionately called in letters, deprived his niece in 1687 of a devoted financial manager and companion of many years in his abbey at Livry, traveling (even though ''traveling with him makes one not so portable''), and the Carnavalet where he too resided. Often negotiator and guarantor himself, his estate continued to bolster the family. But the fate of its securities like those ceded earlier to Mme de Grignan illustrates again the precarious equilibrium and bookkeeping Mme de Sévigné coped with to her last days. Securities transferred to Mme de Grignan in 1683 continued their route to d'Harouys (from whom the Grignans too borrowed several times), then were transferred to his son, Coulanges enjoying the usufruct all the while.[8] After the too generous d'Harouys failed in 1687 and was imprisoned, the Marquise characteristically mixed gratitude and loyalty into her defense of his honor (1.29; 2.19.90). Successors demanded in 1689 an accounting that proved difficult and embarrassing (part of a ''year of infamies'' spilling over into 1690). But final settlement of one consequence of her uncle's death was more harsh.

Livry was lost, with its gardens and woods filled with memories, of Mme de Sévigné's childhood, excursions with Mme de Lafayette and other friends, most of all of her daughter that had made woods and garden speak through their letters. There were other country houses for excursions, Chaulnes, Bâville with the Lamoignons, Brévannes with Mme de Coulanges. But there was no Livry. ''After weeping for the Abbé, I wept for the abbey'' (11.13.87). Despite effort to detach herself from things (10.22.88), the letter-writer goes into perpetual mourning for ''our poor Livry'' (for example, 10.7; 10.9.87; 11.29.88; 4.24.89; 5.25.89; 11.2.89; 1.29.90).

Among the scores of testimonials to edifying preparations for death that continue in the letters, a letter written early one evening in 1688 in the Carnavalet (11.15) has a special place. To Mme de Coulanges's irritation, Mme de Sévigné had given up the country with her to remain at hand during the last illness of Charles de Saint-Aubin, her last surviving Coulanges uncle. He had retired to the Saint-Jacques quarter in whose numerous religious houses so many of her friends spent pious last days.

He was touched to see me, as much as one can be in that quarter. He held my hand a long time and said holy and tender things to me; I was all in tears. It is an occasion not to be lost, to see a man die with Christian peace and tranquility, a detachment, a charity, a desire to be in heaven with God, a holy fear of His judgments but a complete confidence in Christ. It is all divine. That is the quarter in which one must learn to die, if not so fortunate to live there.

The letter-writer's thoughts return in her next letter (11.17) to that room "without noise, calm." A center of conversation at Mme de Lafayette's the day before, it now coexists, death with life, in her letter beside rooms filled by compliments to her grandson's first military distinction and promise of youth. Charles and his wife chose to spend the end of their lives in retirement in the Saint-Jacques quarter. The Marquise did not; but what she had felt there remained with her at Grignan. In the fullest accounts of her death there on April 17, 1696, after ten days' illness (vaguely "continual fever"), which afforded time for her own preparations, the Comte de Grignan wrote to Pomponne and to Moulceau (5.7; 5.28.96) of a strong woman, who possessed the moment in the fullness of her faith. If Mme de Sévigné died alone, her daughter near but not in the last room, it may well have been her own wish and the final severe triumph of sacrifice to God of what she had long felt His.[9]

Resignation to losses of the Coulanges past and the happy Regency beyond her own memories had been made a signpost on the route to new devotion (4.5.80). But even after reaffirmations it suffers harsh testing in the Carnavalet in 1693 with the deaths in the same year of Mme de Lafayette and Bussy. Since one of the most memorable qualities of Mme de Sévigné's letters is their gifts of friendship, the correspondence of more than fifty years' intimate companionship with Mme de Lafayette promises uniquely precious insights. The small number of extant letters is disappointing: one only of the Marquise's and that early (7.24.57) and fifteen to her in twenty years (1672-92). Mme de Lafayette's letters, too, are disappointing. They are a sad abbreviation of the deep understanding that abided in feast and famine through the years, between the celebration of youthful friendship in the 1659 portrait and confirmation of it in the last sentence of her last extant letter: "Believe me, my dearest, you are the person in the world I have most truly loved" (1.24.92).

As Mme de Lafayette admonished her friend (6.30.73), and as close as her letters come to a comment on writing, friendship is not to be judged by the number or volume of letters written. Mme de Sévigné certainly did not. Numerous references to Mme de Lafayette's laconic style, similar in fact to Mme de Grignan's early

style, show that she knew how to read its messages, even as what
little expansive small-talk and fantasy there is in 1673 letters disappears from the unrelieved bleakness of later notes. "You are
old," she wrote (10.8.89) while Mme de Sévigné was wintering at
Les Rochers. Mme de Grignan was shocked by the bluntness, but
her mother took it in good part as the clinching argument (supported by Mmes de Chaulnes and de Lavardin) intended to effect
Mme de Sévigné's reasonable return to Paris from an unhealthful
country winter. Since one corollary was accepting money from
Mme de Chaulnes, and a new debt, Mme de Sévigné preferred her
own reason and "God's will" but paid her tribute to the reason of
friendship behind her friends' scheme (11.29). Mme de Lafayette
was as merciless in contemplating her own "old age" (a year before
her death at fifty-eight). "Alas, my pretty, all I have to say of my
health is bad indeed. In a word, I have rest neither day nor night, in
body or mind. I am no longer a person, through either. . . . It must
finish when God pleases, and I am ready" (1.24.92).

With all she had to remember, Mme de Sévigné's reading of the
last note in which Mme de Lafayette's will to life had ebbed further
doubtless brought tears. There were of course the joys of youth, in
middle age of endless evenings together, shared advice on family
matters, favors indefatigably sought through Mme de Lafayette's
connections and money lent, in short life together that made the
younger woman seem an elder sister. Conversations in her garden,
"the prettiest spot in Paris" (7.24.76), with La Rochefoucauld
were certainly remembered and even there a melancholy that made
the friends seem to her "all but buried." Mme de Lafayette's
debilitation is the more pathetic for the record against which it
plays in letters and memory of her strenuously maintained ambition, efforts on behalf of her family, robust mind, decisive counsel
and actions. The first image of her in the letters after first separation, when strength was sought with her, is of Mme de Lafayette
"alone and afflicted." It is there often, after La Rochefoucauld's
death (4.5.80) or her son's marriage, for example, but not so often
as it may have been in her life, reticent as the letters are on the long
separation from her husband and reserved on that she felt from
God (12.11.89). In the last decade that image, of solitude and
suffering, prevails in the letters.

Mme de Sévigné's eulogy of her friend, addressed to the Comtesse de Guitaut (6.3.93), is unusually expansive (after her hus-

band's death there are ordinarily brief business letters to her) and
defensive. The often-quoted tribute is to "reason in her lifetime
and after her death, that divine reason which was her principal
quality and never left her." But it is not to a life laid out and
lived, we may now see, with the detachment of a rationalist
philosopher, in which religion was treated no differently. Following
a startlingly detailed report of her autopsy, reason in life and death
is the truth of her afflictions, whose languor and "cruel vapors"
were often by others blamed on hypochondria or as willful evasion
of obligations. "I always defended her, when people said she was
mad because she would not go out," Mme de Sévigné insists.
Defending her to the end, the "divine reason always there" pre-
pares for the painful fact of Mme de Lafayette's not receiving the
final sacrament. The letter-writer who in 1680 (6.21) admired the
gift of perseverance in Mme de La Sablière's "true devotion" and
wished it for Mme de Lafayette gives witness to it in the end. "I
have felt on this occasion a sense of religion within me that would
have deepened my grief if I had not been sustained by the hope that
God has been merciful to her." In unembarrassed detail the letter
begun with what had been given, of joy and comfort to her friendship, ends with its last gift and reticence. The life remembered is
and was not felt to be a model of self-sufficiency, but to be
"lacking," deprived of what Mme de Sévigné knew from experience and reflection she had herself abundantly.

Mme de Sévigné's reading of Mme de Lafayette's novel *The
Princess of Cleves* keeps its secrets as tantalizing as scenes of conversation set in her friend's garden but without the three friends'
conversation we are frustrated not to overhear. After one of them,
a sarcastically precious quip may allude to the novel's central scene
of the Princess's confession, perhaps then being discussed (5.30.
72). It suggests that like Bussy and Valincour (whose detailed
critique she praised, 10.12.78) she was more preoccupied with the
scene's credibility than the heroine's agony or the problem of
sincerity it poses, which had so often been the intense concern of
her own early letters. "I'm not surprised that Mme de Clèves loved
Nemours with his fine legs," she again quips with a twinkle of the
Vichy letters in her only reference to the heroine (1.5.89). Two days
after the novel appeared she had read and found it captivating, "a
book that won't be soon forgotten" (3.18.78), and she reread it in
March 1680. Bussy's opinions were immediately solicited; then

after arrival (6.26.78) waited a month for a response that is no more than an "I agree fully with you" (7.27). It is unlikely she did, however, any more than with Bussy's certainty the two of them could have done better, by his invariable criterion, made their principal characters think and speak more naturally (7.23). That *Rabutinage* received no answer. More likely in those terribly tense days with her daughter the letter-writer was too preoccupied with them to wish to prolong discussion or perhaps found that discussion of the novel too close to the bone.

What part Mme de Sévigné and her love played in the genesis of Mme de Lafayette's novel will remain another of the two women's secrets. But analogues in the letter-writer's experience pose themselves, from an incidental question of love (whether a ball should be attended in the loved one's absence) to the central place of the demands and self-demand of reason against passion and the illusory consolation of sincerity, the structuring pattern of retreats and their elusive serenity, and the final imposition of self-knowledge in failure. And if the novel has, as Poulet sees it, "but one aim: to discover the relationship between passion and existence,"[10] so to no lesser degree do Mme de Sévigné's letters of first separation. Her last word on the novel, following the summer in which it was so much discussed, may well be, "Let us live with the living" (10.12.78) and the quotation of Mlle de Scudery on the heart's true measure of love. Both are presuppositions of the last letters and guide self-knowledge in them, when seeing life's "destiny" metaphorically through fictions is like reading novels no longer in season.

With Bussy during the last decade of his life, letter-writing generates none of the old sparks. The bravura, stoic rhetoric of his early exile, after seventeen years in 1683, had aged and allows a place for God (Bussy, 8.4.85; 6.10.88), fusing in a Christian stoicism. Letters are on the way to the moral testament left in his *Discourse on the Proper Use of Adversities*.[11] Mme de Sevigné pays her respect to his "Christian philosophy" (1.6.89), as she had earlier to a philosophy that rather than rigorous stoicism was a gentleman's staple of Horatian wisdom.[12] That was his "experience and nature," Corbinelli complimented him, and Mme de Sévigné left it to him without emulation in her letters. Corbinelli's other compliment, that the cousins' letters equaled Balzac's and Voiture's (12.2.87), did not inspire her either to rewrite her own earliest letters to Bussy.

As before, the letter-writer responds in her own way, of submission, with brief but striking reflections on providence (for example, 12.15.83; 8.13.88). She discusses the war with Bussy, politely attends to his family, keeps him fairly well informed of her comings and goings. She shares sympathetically in his *beaux gestes* of last offers of service to his King (9.22.88; 6.11.90). Moralizing with him, like the smiles of *Rabutinage* that endure to his last letters, remains a pleasure, similar to that of writing Platonizing compliments on enduring friendship to Mlle de Scudéry (9.11.84; No. 995, August 1688). But there is no urgency in it, or in the thirty-five letters written during the decade almost always in response to his (cf. 111 letters to her daughter).

Once, it seems that reflections in the writing may open out a new tension, felt in 1682 (1.23) and later in reduced circumstances (1.8; 3.18.90), the limitation of being a woman. "I am a little wet hen. Sometimes I think: 'But if I had been a man . . . women having permission to be weak, they use it as a privilege' " (10.23.83). Bussy's answer again said it all, to his correspondent, and should say much to us: "If you are weak, Madam, it is because you have been educated to weakness . . . and don't know the strengths of which you are capable" (10.28). Whether from suspicion that Bussy's correspondence would be published with his other prose (cf. 2.15.90), from less sympathy than she expresses, or simply because the best of her mind and strength is again otherwise engaged, the letter-writer ends the long friendship with letters that give much less of herself than what Bussy wished to hear.

The new pattern of life that had made her strength to meet all challenges reveal new capabilities, and makes the last letters what they are, came with Mme de Grignan's return to the Carnavalet in December 1680. Symbolically, she relocated her "study" nearer her mother's room (7.30.89). That return opened a new and last period in the lives of mother and daughter. A period of eight years, before the penultimate separation (seventh) of Mme de Grignan's departure on October 3, 1688, stabilizes realities that satisfy the old dream for the Carnavalet and free the two women from the most dramatic tensions and worst strains of life together that shaped letters from 1671 through 1680.

Mme de Grignan's presence in Paris was required by lawsuits, her son's budding but expensive career in the army, and changes in Grignan's functions in Provence that reduced their income. To her mother's relief as family interests are properly represented, the

Carnavalet became the Grignans' real second residence. It remains at the center of the letter-writer's life, until the last short separation of mother and daughter (the eighth: March 25—May 11, 1694)— "only a moment"—closes the series and the correspondence of mother and daughter (Nos. 1295-1300, 1302). Those calm letters, with last lists of social calls, literary events (among them the exchange of Perrault and Boileau on women), and occupants of an emptied Carnavalet, end with an adieu without regrets to a Paris afflicted by famine and epidemics (5.10.94).

Had her death not broken it, a new pattern of life together was already there in 1694—replacing the alternating presence and absence of Paris and Brittany—which henceforth would have taken Mme de Sévigné regularly with the family between Paris and Grignan. She was welcomed there (November 1690) after her last stay and adieux to Les Rochers (9.17.90) and in 1691 enjoyed the new pleasure of returning to Paris amidst the whole family. In the last two voyages, Grignan becomes her second residence, more surely and fully than when the letter-writer's imagination appropriated it in 1671-72 and she first explored as a visitor the décors of her daughter's new life.[13] Both in Paris and in Provence there was the beginning of a new uninterrupted life together.

With the contentment of shared tenderness and solid friendship, Mme de Sévigné herself could open separations. There was the voyage to Bourbon in 1687 (September-October) when a touch of palsy was feared. But more importantly, a year in Brittany from September 12, 1684, could be undertaken, its letters show, because of the new life in the Carnavalet. The mother was reassured that her daughter would be there to welcome the return to Paris. She knew too that letters need not now strive to create the essential conditions of that welcome.

II   *"Thélème"*

The last two series of letters from Les Rochers, in 1684-85 (Nos. 885-925) and 1689-90 (Nos. 1099-1233), are an unhurried domestic chronicle. Letters of the first stay are an open journal, a daybook of business combined with a personal diary. Its entries in the form of continuing dialogue with Mme de Grignan in Paris benefit in 1684-85 from the shortest delay for delivery of letters in the correspondence and continue without interruption. When during the last stay Mme de Grignan is again in Provence, the letter-journal is amplified but remains essentially unchanged, preserving the shapes of letters and continuity of letter-writing established in 1684.

Momentarily, it seems that the letter-writer may impose upon her new Breton daughter-in-law the comic role forced in earlier letters from Brittany upon Mlle Du Plessis (now mentioned only once in 1689). She indulges in the sketch of a portrait "in negatives" after the fashion of Voiture (10.1.84). But the new Mme de Sévigné, her mother-in-law finds, is neither stiff nor afflicted with a Breton accent. Delicate and serious, without being morose or solemn, she may not make the household "jolly" but does not cast the gloom the letter-writer feared (all the more for her promise to Mme de Grignan to sacrifice imprudent walks). In less than a fortnight's letters, she is again at home and feels qualities of her daughter-in-law that win continuing friendship. Discoveries are recounted of her devotion to Charles, tactful respect for his mother's privacy (and his sister's special place in it), and quiet pleasures in those mother and son had shared. There are some half-amused smiles, of course, but family and neighbors, the society of Rennes and the Estates, provincials and Brittany generally are now left in peace.

With obvious relief, the letter-writer leaves behind the function of entertainer, and is relieved of that of informant. News of the Chaulnes and other old friends in Brittany is sent to Mme de Grignan. News from some half-dozen regular Parisian correspondents, and the Abbe Bigorre's private "news-letters" from the Carnavalet in 1689-90, are relayed to her. But it is Mme de Grignan who now sends the gazettes and her own from Paris and the "tourbillon" of Versailles. "Relations" come with personal progress reports. "You gave me great pleasure talking about Versailles. Mme de Maintenon's place there is unique in the world; there never was or will be anything like it" (9.27.84), her mother responds to the "relation" of an old friend now Queen in all but name (and not the same old friend with whom she had dined in 1673). But again it is preeminently Mme de Grignan's news that is wanted. "Everything that happens in the Carnavalet is my affair, more or less as you take an interest in it" (10.4.84). That is the reality, which reanimates an old expression of love: "In fine, you are the center and cause of everything" (11.26.84).

Settling back into the "little family," the letter-writer pictures herself like a "proper young lady" with her tapestry work, reading, walks at the proper hours, proper attention to estate business and to callers like the Chaulnes, with whom family interest and friendship make her a refreshing and refreshed traveling companion in 1689 (Nos. 1130-39). The peaceful life by the hearth remains the constant background of letter-writing, which elaborates the metaphor of "eating my provisions" that had always translated the economic necessities of life at Les Rochers. Without affectation of a stoicism exhausted in earlier letters, which is moreover no longer responsive to life now with Mme de Grignan, the letter-writer had frankly dreaded and characteristically resigned herself to the new trip: "God has disposed of my destiny and shortly I will have more of the country than I want" (10.1.84). But if "subsisting on my own resources and the little family" (10.4) narrows the mind in one way, as she says, it is opened in another as her letters amplify, refine with a writer's pleasure, and lighten the domestic scene with their descriptions of full days. Empty days of old age darkened by ill health will certainly come, bringing their "humiliating dregs of mind and body" (8.15.85); meanwhile, "I profit with avarice from those God gives me" (10.4.84).

The first winter's letters turn with an autumnal sunshine away from the fireside, then return to its warmth. "Truly, I don't plunge into my old follies; imperceptibly there comes a time when one takes a bit better care of oneself. There is a charming sun for walking, like fine autumn days" (12.27.84). Remembering Christmas with her daughter, who made much of it, warms the letter-writer, the epistolary past enriching its present as the past itself does the present moment of letter-writing. Happiness is before her, visible in what she had wished for Charles, virtual in the capable hands of Mme de Grignan and the "hands of providence" that guide her at Court, keep health bulletins encouraging and special letters coming. In response to those letters, which prolong the Carnavalet, the letter-writer offers her Christmas message: "It is sweet to think I shall never live without you. . . . I see peace in all the hearts I desire it to be."

With that benediction, the letter-writer settles back for a new look at her letters. The "hidden treasure" sought with such avarice in first letter-writing has been discovered, and the old language of love remains. It need not demonstrate or memorialize, but only reveal and then in 1689-90 sustain the equilibrium of the Carnavalet. As at first, it is Mme de Grignan who takes the initiative, not with the metaphors that showed her mother's way to the summer game-letters of 1671 so much as by a running chronicle that literally observes the first maxim of that time's letter-writing: the slightest things about the loved one are precious. But to that ordinary commerce of mother and daughter, Mme de Grignan also brings the "extraordinary" of their relationship, the "inordinate" love of her mother's first letters. From the Carnavalet, Mme de Grignan rewrites her mother's old letters.

After a week, there is the old metaphor of separation like loss of health, to which her mother responds in the spirit of its expression of calm tenderness and of continuity.

I write in peace and repose and, although I am with you, I feel our separation yet very sadly. . . . "You miss me like health," but I disagree. You felt my five or six daily visits and the sweetness of our being together better than health. . . . For me, my dearest, I have nothing on my heart. There was not a moment I didn't feel the pleasure of being with you. . . . The time spent happily with you truly in no way diminished the sharpness of my pleasure. (10.1.84)

The unforced assurances continue to come, reassuring and confirming that the new separation has been only an "interruption." "Of the solid and tender *amitié* [friendship-love] you have for me, I am touched and filled. . . . Ordinarily mothers are not loved as you love me." Thus fulfilled, the roles again reverse; in answer to tenderness, the mother now counsels "passing lightly" over moments that open wounds of separation, then changes the subject. The daughter's gesture of tenderness that had opened a wound repeated the gaze into the loved one's empty room of her mother's first letter in separation. "Why do you give yourself the sword wound of looking into my empty room?" (9.27.84).

The correspondents meet in contemplation of the mother's portrait, as they had in her earlier letters through the daughter's. "I am delighted that you love my portrait," she responded openly to her daughter's appreciation of the smiling serenity of the portrait now at Versailles (11.5). "Look at it sometimes. It is of a mother who adores you, that is, loves you beyond words." It is that portrait, of her mother as she saw her in the Carnavalet, which Mme de Grignan saw again in her mother's letters from 1684 on; "Nicole and Voiture," she wrote of them, to her mother's amusement (2.15.90).

Dissatisfied with her earlier portrait by Le Febvre, which did not
capture all she wished to express in her letters, the new portrait suits
the writer of the letter of November 15, 1684. From her chimney
corner she again recalls warmly one of her daughter's games as a
child, chats happily about friends (the joys of writing to Coulanges
and the trials of Mme de Lafayette, for whom "to be" is so much
more difficult than for the letter-writer at this moment), then looks
forward in this fullness to "hours to oneself" like it. The fullness
of being is enough to lighten the burden of the letter's business,
which "sullies" it, even the reality of "what I possess is no longer
my own." And in this moment of fullness, the "paradigm" of the
letters of the last "period" gives itself to the letter-writer, who
rediscovers with new meaning and ease the victory of the summer
of 1671: that letters need not be *about* anything but ourselves. "We
give first place to what concerns us, and the rest can come to round
off the dispatch."

For the first, in the letters from Brittany of the last two stays
there, it does seem possible to distinguish a paradigm.[14] In earlier
moments, there are representative letters, like the "letter of love's
unreason" or of "sermonizing," shaped as the mind explores and
then closes with them. Patterns also emerge, as letters respond to a
repeated moment, capturing and emphasizing it—to the letter of a
Wednesday, for example; in travel letters; to commemorate private
anniversaries or set introspective balance-sheets. Repetition with
only incidental variations and enhanced by the newly unifying tone
of moderation recurs now, however, regularly enough in the
ordinary ordering of letters that it seems calculated to communicate
the essence of continuity.

Openings now give the "postal facts," with regret for delayed
letters but without crises. Commentary on the style of letters, now
primarily an exchange of compliments, and the daily health bulletin
(until "all the parts are heard from") form a transition, as though
the mother saw health in her daughter's hand as well as heard it in
her tone. The body rounds off the business of the day, the Carnavalet and Les Rochers now merged rather than separated in the
alternating scenes of earlier letters. Transition to the closing returns
to health and commentary on letter-writing, the ultimately important matters before they are enshrined in closings "in beauty"
with the alpha and omega of the old language of love. "I cannot
imagine a love beyond that I feel for you. It would be the 'unknown

lands,' " she closes with a backward glance at the geography of Mlle de Scudéry's "map of the tender" (11.29.84). Or the old lover of Corneille soars: "When one is accustomed to your way of love, all others are laughable. I am very worthy, my *bonne*, of those treasures, by my ability to feel them and the perfect tenderness I have for everything ten leagues around you," then returns to earth: "Let's talk a bit of your health, truthfully, and your affairs" (2.14.85). The conclusion is the echo of the denouement found in the Carnavalet: "You see, my dear child, that you lose nothing on me of your tender and heroic feelings" (12.27.84).

The last metaphor describing the "sweet freedom" of Les Rochers and Mme de Sévigné's letters from Brittany is "Thélème" (6.26; 7.17; 9.18.89), the vision of an antimonastery Renaissance Court with which Rabelais ends his *Gargantua* (Chs. 52-57). Posting the single clause regulating its life—"Do what you will" and with it "holy freedom," the letter-writer effects her last epistolary transformation of a business trip. Under the auspices of the "easy honest company" of the Thelemites sustained by free will and pleasure in their gardens, the "little family" and the Marquise in her woods, Mme de Grignan and family in her "royal château" live their lives in her letters as though at Thélème. "Grace, honor, praise, and light/Are here our sole delight;/Of them we make our song./Our limbs are sound and strong."[15]

"You give me a lovable idea of your days," Mme de Sévigné wrote as she relived the diversions and family happiness at Grignan in her own letters. "What good company! It is agreeable even not to be tempted to leave your terraces. . . . I thank you, my *bonne*, for including me so prettily in your society by telling me everything. . . . God keep you all" (7.13; 10.5.89). Commenting on news from Grignan, following her grandson's budding but expensive career, participating in Pauline's education at home, the letter-writer's principal amplifications in 1689-90 are her "scenes" of life at Grignan and participation in them. "I don't take my sight from my dear Countess, her château, or its occupants" (7.21.89), she shows in every letter. "Although it is not the most important theater in Europe, it is to me," she confesses, then changes the metaphor with the language of Nicole. Assimilated by her imagination and in her letters, the château is now within, "my I" (7.6.89).

In the more frequent elaboration of scenes of solitude at Les Rochers, which constitute the second major amplification of the

1689-90 letters, they are given a special place within the family life
of "perfect and profound repose, peace, silence"—in which "all is
in order and in the order of God" (6.12; 6.15.89). "Don't fear my
solitude," she reassures her daughter as the seasons change from
summer to winter but health remains "perfect." And don't make
too much, she cautions, of a retreat that is in and for that health
"sweet" and "natural"—"I am not an anchorite" (8.21; 9.4;
12.11.89). Letters are "rounded off" with intimate scenes in that
solitude, which in itself is meditative and then elicits more reflection in the writing. Scenes are especially in the woods, which she
found "more serious" (that is, more imposing) on this stay (5.29),
during afternoon walks from five to eight that do not take her too
far down the longest walkway ("The Infinite") or to the most
distant ("The Holy Terror").

> I have a footman who follows me, I have books, I change spots and vary
> my paths. A book of devotion and another of history; I alternate, for
> diversion. Meditate a little on God, on His providence; possess one's soul;
> think of the future. Finally at eight, sometimes a bit far away, I hear the
> supper bell. I join the Marquise [her daughter-in-law] in her fine garden.
> We make up a company together for a twilight supper. (6.29)

"Is this solitude not right for a person who must think of herself
and is, or wishes to be, a Christian?" she asks in closing, with
tenderness that is now the easy companion of this appropriate
account of her time. Ritually, "three hours, alone with God,
myself, you, your letters and my book," this "solitude, profound
silence, this freedom" (7.6.89), are made a last gift of fullness to
her daughter.

Devotion takes its place in the full life as easily and appropriately
as daily Mass in the chapel or the "good books" that continue to be
for the Marquise, as for Montaigne, "honest amusements or . . .
the learning that treats of the knowledge of myself and instructs me
in how to die well and live well."[16] Montaigne himself was an "old
friend," the letter-writer proclaimed after rediscovering in his essay
"Of the Love of Fathers for their Children" (II.8) his endorsement
of the expression of paternal affection to children (10.6.79).
Montaigne's book, criticized by both Jansenists and Malebranche
for self-indulgent vanity and skepticism but a favorite of Mme de
Grignan, is not on the recommended list for Pauline (1.15.90), a list

that comprises the Marquise's fragmentary essay "On Books." He is not a chosen companion either at Les Rochers or in the "learning," in his sense of the word, of the Marquise's last letters.[17] In like manner, she resists another extreme, mystical texts recommended by Corbinelli (9.11.89).

Finding with Charles that a mystical text on prayer is "incomprehensible" (1.8.90), they return to their usual fare of readings, including old friends: Nicole's continued essays, recommended to and liked by Pauline; Le Tourneux's *Rules of the Christian Life* (10.26.89; begun in February); Godeau's last volume in his history of the Church (11.16.89 through 1.4.90); Fléchier's *Life of the Great Theodosius*, also recommended for Pauline (11.27.89); Pascal's *Provincial Letters*, which will sharpen her granddaughter (12.21.89); Arnauld and Nicole's *Perpetuity of the Faith* (1.25.90); Saint John Chrysostom's *Homilies* (2.19; 2.26.90) and Augustine's *Letters*, which Mme de Grignan was reading (6.25.90); Abbadie's theology that with Godeau's history is a "delicious marriage of voice and lute" (12.21.89).

Among new arrivals, always history and memoirs when not moral philosophy or theology, the most admired are the Jansenist Jean Hamon's *On Continual Prayer* (7.10; 10.26.89) and Bossuet's *History of the Variations of the Protestant Churches* (6.1; 6.26; 11.23.89). In that compendium of orthodoxy, Mme de Sévigné found, as she affirms after reading the Protestant Abbadie, a reaffirmed "truth of my own religion." With it, there is no need to condemn novels. If they have no place now at Les Rochers, they may at Grignan. Why shouldn't Pauline read novels? "I used to love them, and I haven't run my course too badly. . . . Mme de Lafayette is still another example" (11.16.89). And why not Corneille's comedies and *Polyeucte* and *Cinna*? (5.5.89). "It is not easy to spoil a healthy mind." (And is Pauline having any geography or science, her grandmother inquires, obviously wishing her to be educated to strength.) Staying the course at Les Rochers, the letter-writer smiles at the arrival of a new translation of Augustine's *On True Religion*. Already well fortified, "with Abbadie, Pascal, and the *History of the Church* [Godeau's], we are already prepared to suffer martyrdom; at least we think so, firm as our minds are" (1.29.90).

If the books read in the little family reach the letters, it is in response to the repeated question, "What are you reading?"

(11.23.89). Their "learning," maintaining a constant if not continual devotion (with a notable number of books on prayer, which
was a "problem" in 1680), responds humbly to a new posing of the
question asked after Vichy—"Are you devout?" The response is
the same, a "No, but. . . ." "I do know my religion. . . . What is
good from what only appears so. I hope I do not err and that God
continues to show me my good. The graces of the past give me hope
for those to come, and accordingly I live with confidence, but one
mixed with a good dose of fear" (1.15.90). Conversation on
Pauline's education develops naturally into dialogue on her grandmother's and continues to do so, since Mme de Grignan's religion
is as sure (6.22.89) as her mind is "luminous" in its expositions of
Descartes (9.28.89). She is a perfect guide for Pauline (for example,
1.18.90), and with her concern she is the perfect interlocutor for her
mother. It is for them both that a last fine letter opening from new
reading of Nicole, in a scene of solitude (7.13.89), offers the
Marquise's "last word" on providence.

For my providence, I could not live in peace without contemplating it
often. It is the consolation of the sad states of life, it cuts short all outcries,
it calms all pains, it fixes all thought; that is, it should, were we wise
enough. . . .

Mme de Grignan is also the perfect listener for the generalities
that arise from this experience, which like Montaigne's in his final
essay substitutes for the ideal of the mind's fullness and mediates in
the absence of its full control. The expanded pleasures of the letter-
writer-moralist have their place among the amplifications of the
1689-90 letters. "Men like change . . .," she reflects, shortly after a
"men like command . . ." (10.23; 10.19.89); "I am still alone and
am not bored. I have my health, books . . . one can indeed go far
with a little reason mixed into all that." The moralist does go
further: "Truly, the King deserves all that is done for him, but one
must confess also that he is well served. That service is the image we
should have of serving God, or rather it is thus that one should
serve Him. . . . Alas, you are right indeed, my daughter; that
providence which we talk about so well scarcely serves in those
things that grip our hearts. We are wrong, but in all we feel our
weakness . . ." (8.2.89). Feeling it, the letter-writer continues in her
own voice—and with the echoes of her daughter's—to speak well

of providence.

In the constant but discreet amplifications of health bulletins there is always some fitting acknowledgment by the letter-writer of God's blessing. Any epistolary conversation about Louis-Provence and his mother's dedication to his career or about Pauline and her "becoming a little person" has its "God keep you all"—"That is my ordinary refrain" (7.10.89), which lives easily with quotations from Benserade, La Fontaine, or a satirical song of Mme de Grignan's that happily echoes the music of Grignan (7.17). From the old storming of providence, and with the new vigilance, there remains a perpetual "God wishes it thus"—"always my refrain, I know no other, save that I shall love you perfectly and eternally" (6.19.89).

In their fullness, the letters from Brittany in 1684-85 and 1689-90, rather than the brief correspondence of 1694 or letters to others during the last stay at Grignan,[18] are the real conclusion of the correspondence of mother and daughter. Revealing and maintaining the friendship that was the new and final "lease on life" of the Carnavalet from December 1680, and anticipating the happiness of life together that replaces letter-writing at Grignan, the letters from Brittany project a last illusion of Mme de Sévigné's epistolary art. And in doing so, they epitomize the quality of its transcendence.

"My letter is infinite, like the love I have for you" (9.14.89), the letter-writer confesses with her pleasures of the letter-journal, four months after she had looked back to the happiness of the Carnavalet and admitted with a Moliéresque smile: "I became so pleasantly used to you that I had forgotten I knew how to make prose" (7.10.89). The "infinite letter," translating the Thélème metaphor, is the final illusion. In the letter-journal, the "adieux" mark an interruption, not a separation. Letters are no longer self-contained fragments of special consolation, symbolic of a fragmented life. They are the installments in one unending letter contextual with the daily life whose continuity it both records and provides.

CHAPTER 7

Conclusion

THE proper inheritor of Mme de Sévigné's letters is first her daughter who preserved them. Her own letters, especially to her children, come to resemble her mother's, more than the society letter-writing of a Mme de Coulanges. More too than for the readers of eighteenth-century secretaries of letter-writing, from which the Marquise's "natural letters" began to offer lessons, they preserve a model for the daughter whose life was also devoted to her family. After her mother's death ended the long dialogue on differences, then after her son's premature death, her life, like her mother's, turns in its own way inward and to greater devotion.[1]

Genealogists (also prescient *Sévignistes*) find the Marquise's epistolary legacy still in the letters of her great-granddaughter, Sophie de Vence-Villeneuve. It is there as surely in Mme de Genlis's and a generation of readers who found their style in Perrin's edition of the Marquise's letters as well as in the pages of Rousseau's *The New Heloise*.[2] The heritage of the "Queen Mother of letter-writers" is given the imperial cachet by another natural writer, who also found consolation and pleasure in writing to her "dearest child." In Queen Victoria's letter-writing, the same tendernesses, counsel, finally "God's will be done," watch over the Princess Royal's first years of marriage that preside over Mme de Grignan's in her mother's first love letters.

Everyone says how well you behave—how good, quiet, civil and dignified your manner is! How thankful and happy do we feel! How right your sometimes not very patiently and kindly listened to Mama was, when she told you, you could do everything, if you would but take pains, control yourself and conquer all little difficulties—as you had such great qualities, such a heart of gold! And so it is, my beloved child. . . .[3]

If Simone de Beauvoir has found in the Marquise an exemplary freedom, the privilege only of aristocratic women in her society, social historians may also find in the world of the letters ample evidence of the wretchedness of an estate that separated mothers and daughters in mutual hostilities.[4] It now seems impossible to enshrine "mother beauty" in the "poetry of the family" Lamartine and his generation created or the idealized motherhood of Balzac's *Béatrix*. But it is equally impossible to find in the letters a Mme de Sévigné who is a Balzacian "monster of maternity." "Mother beauty" exists exceptionally, at one extreme of a spectrum that extended at the other to the Marquise de Brinvilliers, whose murdered daughter was a sacrifice to her own happiness. Mme de Sévigné's letters keep the chronicle of other sacrifices and the beauty of the celebration of a friendship that in letter-writing pursued the enlightened struggle for liberating autonomy of mother and daughter.

Long valued and used by historians (including guides who keep the Marquise alive for visitors of Paris's Marais quarter), the Marquise's "memoirs" distill and convey the life of surfaces, sensibilities, and spirit of three decades of Louis XIV's reign. Her view of the world from the Carnavalet, through her sensibility and imagination, impressionist observation and vividly told anecdotes, may not open it as Dickens's letters do his. But those qualities with her distance on events, moralist's critical judgments, and the special interests of her art of letter-writing capture her world as Proust does his "by Guermantes' way." However powerfully that creation of the letters has been felt, it is the love story in letters that has haunted readers, who continue to feel its drama as Racinian and in it poetry of transcending permanence.

Not only La Rochefoucauld saw in Mme de Sévigné's letters and life the anatomy of the effects and dependencies of love. Mme de Lafayette, too, at the inception of her novel and during the genesis of *The Princess of Cleves*, saw her friend's search for autonomy in solitude, testings of reason and sincerity, and her combats with time and its sacrifices. Had Rousseau been reading the "frivolities" he dismissed new books to be when the Perrin edition appeared, he might have found in the Marquise's letters a drama of separation and loss not unlike that of his novel *The New Heloise*. But for other novelists, the realities of her correspondence were a rich repository. Its dependence on the "vicissitudes of the post" and its acute sense of time both in its disintegrating flux and its persistent patterns, among other qualities, nourish the development of the "novel by letters." [5]

The fullness created in Mme de Sévigné's letter-writing in absence—which can no longer be seen as the place of betrayal and extinction of love of Guilleragues's *Portuguese Letters*—found its poet in Lamartine. The letters from the woods of Les Rochers merge in his readings of them with his own poetry. Its analyst is Proust. In his novel, Mme de Sévigné is the motif of the grandmother, then associated with the narrator himself. She becomes a mediating symbol of the artist, placed with the painter Elstir among those whose art gives new ways of seeing. [6] Seen through the novel, the Marquise's letters with their "unreasonable love," and their avid quest for knowledge of the "loved one"—and ever receding hopes for total possession—evoked by their poetry seem fully Proust's Swann in love. But her answer to the Proustian question —is absence not the fullest and most consoling of presences?—is a resounding negative, despite all the temptations of privileged moments of letter-writing.

Mme de Sévigné's essential adventure was not the timelessness of art. It was a material correspondence, changing in time but constant, the adventure of the "infinite letter" but also of the one everchanging but enduring "true letter," that letter Virginia Woolf desired to be "as a film of wax pressed close to the graving of the mind." [7] As those "true letters" from her daughter call forth her own, bringing the writer into full possession of herself, the final drama of the correspondence is twofold. As for the Princess of Cleves, it is the progressive discovery and mastery of a personal language. The fullness of that language then brings with the consciousness of its limitations a dialogue on the tragic implications of the fact of humanity and the mind's fragile power to deal with its limitations. [8] That dialogue Mme de Sévigné shares with the greatest "classical" writers of her age.

In the fullness of her letters—with their diversity, richness, openness, and joy of life—Mme de Sévigné finds a transcendence of life through writing that is exceptional for the great writers of her time. The woman Marie de Rabutin-Chantal who began accidentally to write ends, through writing, as the very type of the writer. The beauty, persuasiveness, and desire for life through communication of her text become her beauty, her being, her life. In the general gloom of visions of diminished power and reduced life of the great literary texts of her time, the Mme de Sévigné of the letters still communicates—as Wagner heard Mozart—"music's genius of love and light."

Notes and References

Place of publication is Paris unless otherwise designated.

Preface

1. All parenthetical references, by date (month, day, year) or number, follow the datings and numberings established by Roger Duchêne's edition. Translations are my own.

Chapter One

1. *Œuvres de Sainte-Chantal*. Edition authentique (1875-1893), VII, 239.

2. Pearls always in portraits were doubtless worn with memories of her: for her estate, J. Lemoine, *Mme de Sévigné, sa famille et ses amis* (1926), p. 94.

3. Cf. R. Duchêne, "Une Reconnaissance excessive?" *XVIIe Siècle* 74 (1967): 27-53.

4. *La Femme et la société française dans la première moitié du XVIIe siècle* (1929), pp. 46-48.

5. B. Magné, "Humanisme et culture féminine au XVIIe siècle." *Marseille* 95 (1973): 47-51.

6. For his theories, B. Bray, ed., *Soixante-dix-sept lettres inédites* (The Hague, 1966), pp. 46-55.

7. *Vie*, Sainte-Chantal, *Œuvres* (1862), I, 352.

8. E. Stopp views the scene as Rabutin theatrics. *Madame de Chantal* (London, 1962), pp. 109-12.

9. See R. Devos, *Vie religieuse, féminisme et société, l'origine social des Visitandines* (Annecy, 1973).

10. For many financial details, *Documents du Minutier Central* (1960), pp. 330-69.

11. Charles's appraisal (9.27.96), Duchêne, III, 1697-98.

12. See A. L. Moote, *The Revolt of the Judges* (Princeton, 1971), pp. 38-40, 78, 81, 180, passim.

13. *Œuvres*, ed. R. Ternois (1962), I, 53; E. Kossmann, *La Fronde* (Leiden, 1954), pp. 140-44.

14. See J. H. M. Salmon, *Cardinal de Retz* (London, 1969), pp. 369-71, passim.

15. Tallemant, *Historiettes*, ed. A. Adam (1961), II, 429; Bussy,

Histoire amoureuse, ed. A. Adam (1967), pp. 149-50.

16. E. Magne, *Ninon de Lanclos* (*sic*) (1925), pp. 87-90; Tallemant, "Mme de Gondran," II, 430-31.

17. H. Bourde de la Rogerie, "Terres et seigneuries de la famille de Sévigné," *Mémoires de la Société d'histoire et d'archéologie de Bretagne* 7 (1926): 299-323.

Chapter Two

1. On portraits, J. Wilhelm, "Un portrait de Mme de Sévigné," *Bulletin du Musée Carnavalet* 20 (1967): 3-19. Almost all reproduced in *Marseille* 95 (1973).

2. *Clelia*, trans. J. Davies (London, 1678), p. 361.

3. Cf. B. Treloar, "What is Preciosity?" *Les Précieuses ridicules* (London, 1970), p. 12.

4. Seeing evidence of sapphism here is anachronistic misreading of the compliment.

5. D. Mayer, "Le Portrait de Mme de Sévigné par Mme de Lafayette," *XVIIᵉ Siècle* 101 (1972): 72-87.

6. See commentary by S. Haig, *Madame de Lafayette* (New York, 1970), pp. 15-19.

7. E. Avigdor, "La vraie préciosité d'une véritable précieuse," *XVIIᵉ Siècle* 108 (1975): 59-74.

8. Voiture, *Lettres* (Amsterdam, 1709), I, 1 (ca. 1635).

9. *Lettres*, I, 231 (10.27.38).

10. See E. B. O. Borgerhoff, *The Freedom of French Classicism* (Princeton, 1950), pp. 94; 14-15, on "agrément."

11. *Lettres*, I, 199 (s.d.).

12. For roles, C. I. Silin, *Benserade and His Ballets de cour* (Baltimore, 1940), pp. 315, 317, 321, 334, 348.

13. *Lettres*, I, 293 (1642); 233 (11.25.38), 253 (9.10.40).

14. Striking examples of personalized business, condolence, recommendation letters, R. Duchêne, *Réalité vécue et art épistolier*, pp. 28-34; manuals listed, pp. 391-94.

15. Both contracted misalliances.

16. Verbal fantasy; she was eight at the time.

17. *Mémoires*, trans. P.E.P. (1829; rpt. London, 1895), I, 185.

18. B. Guyon, "Prolégomènes à une édition critique des Lettres de Mme de Sévigné," *Marseille* 95 (1973): 31.

Chapter three

1. G. Mongrédien, *L'Affaire Foucquet* (1956), p. 108; J. Wolf, *Louis XIV* (New York, 1968) p. 375.

2. Once attributed to Molière. See Mongrédien, pp. 155-68.

3. R. Jasinski, *La Fontaine et le premier recueil des Fables* (1965), I, 96, 86-96, passim.

4. Duchêne, I, 56, n. 2.

5. J. Orieux, *Bussy Rabutin* (1958), p. 29.

6. See C. Rouben, "Un jeu de société du grand siècle," *XVIIe Siècle* 97 (1972): 97-98.

7. Orieux, p. 50.

8. *Histoire amoureuse*, p. 43.

9. Extended analysis by C. Garaud, "Qu'est-ce que le rabutinage," *XVIIe Siècle* 93 (1971): 27-53.

10. See C. Rouben, "Histoire et géographie galante du grand siècle," *XVIIe Siècle* 93 (1971): 56-61.

11. F. Nies, "Quelques aspects lexicaux dans les lettres de Madame de Sévigné," *Marseille* 95 (1973): 15.

12. Exaggeration shows fear of gossip; no translation yet.

13. See G. Mongrédien, "Un ami de Mme de Sévigné," *Mercure* 304 (1948): 222-35.

14. Quoted by Duchêne, I, 103, n. 3; 105, n. 11.

15. Duchêne, I, 105, n. 4.

16. Duchêne, "Affaires d'argent et affaires de famille au XVIIe siècle," *XVIIe Siècle* 53 (1961): 3-20.

17. *Les sept couches de Mme de Grignan* (1935); *Mme de Sévigné*, pp. 113-16.

Chapter Four

1. Malherbe, sonnet to Mme d'Auchy. Thanking Ménage for a Malherbe, she promised "to profit from it and decorate my mind with all sorts of fine things" (No. 25, 1654).

2. Cf. on "psychasthenic distortion," M. Foucault, *Mental Illness and Psychology* (New York, 1976), pp. 24, 48, 53.

3. "My good girl," hallmark, personal endearment.

4. Cf. Duchêne, *Mme de Sévigné* (1968), pp. 22-24, 103.

5. Duchêne, I, 199, n. 1.

6. Quoted by Foucault, *Madness and Civilization* (New York, 1973), p. 120.

7. On metacommentary, B. Bray, "L'Epistolière au miroir," *Marseille* 95 (1973): 23-29.

8. See Duchêne, I, 173, n. 4.

9. Cf. Duchêne, I, 156, n. 1; Proust, *A la recherche du temps perdu* (Pléiade ed.), III, 141.

10. See Duchêne, "Lettres et gazettes au XVIIe siècle," *RHMC* 18 (1971): 489-502.

11. Quoted by Duchêne, I, 158, n. 6.
12. See Duchêne, *Réalité vécue,* pp. 284, 293.
13. For a more systematic inventory (with different conclusions), M. Gérard, "Molière dans la correspondance de Mme de Sévigné," *RHLF* 73 (1973): 608-25.
14. See W. G. Moore, "Molière's Theory of Comedy," *L'Esprit créateur* 6 (1966): 137-44.
15. See C. Lougee, *Le Paradis des femmes* (Princeton, 1976), pp. 163-64; Duchêne, I, 271.
16. Cf. Duchêne, I, 284, n. 4.
17. I, 263, n. 3 (6.7.71); 276, n. 4 (6.21.71).

Chapter Five

1. v. 28: "Un seul être me manque et tout est dépeuplé."
2. Reconstructed by Duchêne, II, 1368-69; see also M. Gallet and B. de Montgolfier, "L'Hôtel Carnavalet," *Bulletin du Musée Carnavalet* 27 (1974).
3. Cf. P. Ariès, *Essais sur l'histoire de la mort en occident* (1975), pp. 19, 48-49.
4. *Journals,* trans. J. O'Brien (New York, 1947), I, 270.
5. J. Calvet, *Les Idées morales de Mme de Sévigné* (1909), pp. 23-32; H. Busson, *La Religion des classiques.*
6. Duchêne places the moment later, 3.13.80 (II, 872, n. 4), inexplicably in view of 1677 letters.
7. Mme de Sévigné knew only the Port-Royal edition of Pascal's *Pensées* (rpt. Saint-Etienne, 1971). See Section V.
8. "On Self-Knowledge," Chapter III. "On Self-Love," continuing it, seems to her "luminous" (12.15.75).
9. His influence may seem still overestimated by E. Avigdor, *Mme de Sévigné* (1974), pp. 192, 193-201. Cf. on the evolution of her views, Duchêne, II. 188, n. 1.
10. On these letters (1681-96) and their "care," M. Gérard, "Les lettres de Mme de Sévigné au président Moulceau," *RHLF* 74 (1974: 474-82.
11. Traditional praise, for example, Aubénas, *Mémoires sur Mme de Sévigné* (1865), pp. 139ff; Gérard-Gailly, pp. 158ff.
12. Quoted by A. de Bennetot, *Mme de Sévigné aux eaux de Vichy* (Vichy, 1966), pp. 19-20.
13. Bennetot, p. 30.
14. Busson, p. 37.
15. Cf. Avigdor, pp. 203-208 and passim.

16. No. 205 (the "dungeon") figures prominently in the Port-Royal edition (rpt. 1971, p. 12).

17. *Mmé de Sévigné* (1968), p. 99.

18. Excluded in Port-Royal ed. Brunschvicg Nos. 252, 245, refining these notes and their spirit, are included (pp. 60, 380).

19. Duchêne, *Mme de Sévigné* (1968), pp. 48-49.

20. Cf. V. Brombert, "Pascal's Happy Dungeon," *YFS* 38 (1967): 230-42.

21. Ed. J. Chéné and J. Pintard (1962), pp. 527ff; cf. pp. 653ff. On her edition, Duchêne, II, 938, n. 2.

22. For a just account, H. Allentuch, *Mme de Sévigné* (Baltimore, 1962), pp. 103-106.

23. Cf. H. M. Davidson, "Conflict and Resolution in Pascal's *Pensées,*" *RR* 49 (1958): 115-18.

Chapter Six

1. "Mme de Sévigné" (1829), *Portraits de femmes* (Garnier ed., s.d.), p. 15.

2. See Preface.

3. R. Duchêne, "Partage des biens et partage des affections: Mme de Sévigné et ses enfants," *Annales de l'Université Aix-Marseille* 44 (1969): 172-76.

4. Ibid., pp. 160-62.

5. For a spirited account of campaigns and courtships, see Gérard-Gailly, pp. 121-36.

6. R. Duchêne, "Affaires d'argent et affaires de famille au XVIIᵉ siècle: Mme de Sévigné et Guillaume d'Harouys," *XVIIᵉ Siècle* 53 (1961): 13.

7. For slightly different interpretation of the letter, cf. Duchêne, "Partage des biens," p. 168.

8. R. Duchêne, "Affaires d'argent," p. 16.

9. For rigorous discussion of all it now seems possible to know of the "last separation" and death, see J. Cordelier, "Mme de Sévigné seule devant la mort," *Marseille* 95 (1973): 71-82; 79, 81 on Saint-Aubin.

10. *Studies in Human Time* (Baltimore, 1956), p. 131. On the novel and the letters, see J. Cordelier, *Mme de Sévigné par elle-même* (1967), pp. 65-69 and passim.

11. Cf. C. Rouben, *Bussy-Rabutin épistolier* (1974), pp. 180-91.

12. See J. Marmier, *Horace en France au XVIIᵉ siècle* (1962), pp. 84-85, 376-77; Rouben, pp. 194-97.

13. See R. Duchêne, "Les Provençaux de Mme de Sévigné," *Marseille* 95 (1973): 99-104.

14. For an essay of definition of a different kind of paradigm, cf. B. Bray, "Quelques aspects du système épistolaire de Mme de Sévigné," *RHLF* 69 (1969): 491-505.

15. Rabelais, *Gargantua and Pantagruel,* trans. J. M. Cohen (Baltimore, 1955), p. 154.

16. "On Books" (I.10), *The Complete Works,* trans. D. Frame (Stanford, 1948), p. 297.

17. Not more than four significant allusions in all, always by heart and always as embellishment, indicate Montaigne was never a formative influence on her thought in maturity.

18. On those letters, R. Duchêne, "Les Provençaux," p. 102; J. Cordelier, "Mme de Sévigné seule devant la mort," pp. 74-76 and passim.

Chapter Seven

1. Her letters, in *Lettres de Mme de Sévigné,* ed. Monmerqué (1862), X; "On Fénelon. . . ," ibid., XI, 292-94.

2. The principal sale catalogues of private libraries in the last quarter of the eighteenth century invariably list one of the Perrin editions.

3. *Dearest Daughter: Letters between Queen Victoria and the Princess Royal, 1858-1861* (New York, 1964), pp. 36-37.

4. *The Second Sex,* trans. H. Parshley (New York, 1952), pp. 119, 133; cf. D. Hunt, *Parents and Children in History* (New York, 1972), pp. 121-25.

5. See J. Altman, *Epistolarity: Approaches to a Form* (Columbus, 1981).

6. A. Labat, "Proust's Mme de Sévigné," *L'Esprit créateur* 15 (1975): 271-85.

7. *Letters,* ed. N. Nicholson (New York, 1975), I, 282.

8. Cf. on Mme de Lafayette, W. G. Moore, *French Classical Literature: An Essay* (Oxford, 1961), p. 61.

Selected Bibliography

Because of the availability of only incomplete editions of Mme de Sévigné's letters, older general studies (and popularizations based on them through the 1950s) often give incorrect information and are subject to caution also in interpretation. Only sources in French and English are listed. For general bibliography see:

CABEEN, DAVID C. *A Critical Bibliography of French Literature.* Vol. III, Supplement, ed. H. G. Hall. Syracuse: Syracuse University Press. To appear (1982).

CIORANESCU, ALEXANDRE. *Bibliographie de la littérature française au dix-septième siècle.* Vol. III. Paris: C.N.R.S., 1967.

PRIMARY SOURCES

Lettres, ed. E. Gérard-Gailly. Paris: Gallimard, Pléiade. 3 Vols. (1953-1963). First collective ed. using all MSS. (1,155 letters). Brilliant, polemical introduction.

Correspondance, ed. Roger Duchêne. Paris: Gallimard, Pléiade. Vol I, 1646-75 (1972); Vol II, 1675-July 1680 (1973); Vol III (1978). First fully critical ed. Long essay on MSS. and early eds. (I, pp. 755-830). Rich biographical, historical, stylistic annotation gives much new information. Extensive redating and textual correction of Gérard-Gailly ed.

Lettres, ed. Bernard Raffali. Paris: Garnier-Flammarion, 1976. Useful collection of 165 letters (with Gérard-Gailly text); introduction stresses literary achievement.

Selected Letters, trans. H. T. Barnwell. London: Everyman, 1960. Well chosen, translated, and annotated.

SECONDARY SOURCES[1]

Studies by E. Bachellier, E. Badinter, B. Beugnot (1980), L. Horowitz (1981), G. B. Menscher added here appeared while this book was in press.

ALLENTUCH, HARRIET. *Mme de Sévigné: A Portrait in Letters.* Baltimore: Johns Hopkins, 1963. Best and most complete portrait in English. Uses characterology revealingly.

AVIGDOR, EVA. *Mme de Sévigné: un portrait intellectuel et moral.* Paris: Nizet, 1975. Exploratory essay seeking constants that could modify traditional views of spiritual evolution.

159

BACHELLIER, EVELYNE. "De la conversation à la conversion," *Communications* 30 (1979): 31-56. Explores the dichotomy "conversation/causerie" that "subsumes" those of "galanterie/amour (-passion)" and "esprit/coeur." Suggestive psychological commentary.

BADINTER, ELISABETH. *L'Amour en plus. Histoire de l'amour maternel, XVIIe-XXe siècle*. Paris: Flammarion, 1980. Study of seventeenth-century family ("L'Amour absent") and maternal indifference provides a background highlighting the exceptional nature of Mme de Sévigné's letters.

BEUGNOT, BERNARD. "Débats autour du genre épistolaire." *Revue d' Histoire littéraire de la France* 74 (1974): 195-202. Useful résumé of questions of spontaneity vs. artistic control.

BEUGNOT, BERNARD. "Madame de Sévigné telle qu'en elle-même enfin?" *French Forum* 5 (1980): 207-17. Analysis of contributions of Duchêne edition and of questions yet open to research and interpretation.

BRAY, BERNARD. "Quelques aspects du système épistolaire de Mme de Sévigné," *Revue d'Histoire littéraire de la France* 69 (1969): 491-505. Important and controversial treatment of epistolarity and tentative setting of paradigms.

CHOLEAU, JEAN. *Le grand coeur de Mme de Sévigné*. Vitré: Unvaniez Arvor, 1959. Violent polemical diatribe, useful if corrected elsewhere, as repertory of negatives.

CORDELIER, JEAN. *Mme de Sévigné par elle-même*. Paris: Editions du Seuil, 1965. Most lively and dramatic presentation, sensitive to literary qualities and resonances of them from Mme de Lafayette to Proust.

DILLEMAN, G., and H. LEMAY, "Les médicaments de Mme de Sévigné," *Revue d'Histoire de la Pharmacie* 18 (1966): 1-58. Definitive, documented treatment of knowledge and practice of medications.

DUBOIS, E. T. "Mme de Sévigné et l'Angleterre," *Dix-Septième Siècle* 93 (1971): 75-97. Appreciations from Horace Walpole to Virginia Woolf, with many less well known.

DUCHENE, ROGER. *Mme de Sévigné*. Paris: Desclée de Brouwer, "Les Ecrivains devant Dieu," 1968. Presentation of spiritual evolution. Refocuses but does not supersede study by Henri Busson *(La Religion des classiques*, 1948).

————. *Réalité vécue et art épistolaire: Mme de Sévigné et la lettre d'amour*. Paris: Bordas, 1970. Authoritative biography and study of genesis of letters. Most complete discussion of history and practice of seventeenth-century letter-writing. Extensive treatment of manuals of letter-writing, collections of letters. Information on the postal system nowhere else available. Best overall treatment.

————. "Réalité vécue et réussite littéraire: le statut particulier de la lettre," *Revue d'Histoire littéraire de la France* 71 (1971): 177-94. Useful résumé, reflections on longer study.

————. "Du destinataire au public, ou les métamorphoses d'une correspondance," *Revue d'Histoire littéraire de la France* 76 (1976): 29-46.

————. "Signification du romanesque; l'exemple de Mme de Sévigné," *Revue d'Histoire littéraire de la France* 77 (1977): 578-96. Analysis of intensifications of experience by the romanesque, constant throughout the letters.

GERARD-GAILLY, EMILE. *Madame de Sévigné.* Paris: Hachette, 1971. Collection of pioneering studies, published 1926-67, on biography, family, friends, images of successive editions. Often purposely idiosyncratic and provocative. Documentation omitted; numerous errors of fact and printing. Extensive and unique bibliography.

HOROWITZ, LOUISE. "Madame de Sévigné," *Love and Language: A Study of the Classical French Moralist Writers.* Columbus: Ohio State

————. "The Correspondence of Madame de Sévigné: Lettres ou Belles-Lettres," *French Forum* 6 (1981): 13-27. Valuable assessment of problems of generic and literary definition of the letters with a reading of their self-portraiture in a "closed text."
University Press, 1977, pp. 91-111. Suggestive treatment of language as choice of means of structuring life through writing.

HOWARD, CATHERINE. *Madame de Sévigné en France au dix-huitième siècle.* Unpublished Ph.D. Dissertation, Stanford University (*DAI* 37 [1977]: 7777A). First systematic history of literary reputation, from Bussy's and Mme de Grignan's appreciations to the Revolution. Excludes consideration of literary influences.

JOUHANDEAU, MARCEL. "La vraie Sévigné," *Ecrits de Paris*, September 1959, pp. 76-84. Vigorous counterstatement to the determinism of Freudian interpretation and the debate on it launched by Gérard-Gailly ed., stressing freedom and spontaneity.

LABAT, ALVIN. "Proust's Mme de Sévigné," *L'Esprit Créateur* 15 (1975): 271-85. Penetrating discussion of Proust's appreciation of style, passion, and time in the letters and their place in his novel.

LANSON, GUSTAVE. *Choix de Lettres du XVIIe siècle.* 7th ed. Paris: Hachette, 1904. Seminal, still useful introductory essay on aesthetics of letter-writing. The collected letters and commentary remain an illuminating context for appreciation of Mme de Sévigné's distinctive place among contemporary letter-writers and in epistolary traditions.

LEMOINE, JEAN. *Madame de Sévigné, sa famille et ses amis.* Paris: Hachette, 1926. Carefully documented and interpreted biography to marriage.

Marseille 95 (1973). Twelve papers from 1972 colloquium at Marseilles, illustrated with a fine collection of portraits. Important contributions by B. Bray (on style), J. Cordelier (on death), J. Deprun (Cartesianism), F. Nies (language and inventiveness).

MENSCHER, GAIL B. *Problems of Time and Existence in the Letters of Madame de Sévigné*. Unpublished Ph.D. Dissertation, University of Iowa (*DAI* 38 [1978]: 4200-01A).

MUNK, GERDA. *Mme de Sévigné et Mme de Grignan*. Utrecht: Schotanus en Jens, 1966. Essential critical evaluation of sentimental traditions, myths surrounding mother and daughter. Most complete portrait and defense of Mme de Grignan, superseding studies by Taillandier (1938), Murbach (1939).

NICOLICH, ROBERT. "Life as Theatre in the *Lettres* of Madame de Sévigné," *Romance Notes* 16 (1974): 676-82.

ROUBEN, CESAR. *Bussy-Rabutin épistolier*. Paris: Nizet, 1974. Most complete study of the correspondence, unique in its volume, literary qualities, and vantage points for viewing Mme de Sévigné.

TILLEY, ARTHUR. *Madame de Sévigné: Some Aspects of Her Life and Character*. Cambridge: The University Press, 1936. Dated but perceptive essays on Mme de Sévigné and the "news," her friends, books, and life at Les Rochers.

VIGOUROUX, MONIQUE. *Le thème de la retraite et de la solitude chez quelques épistoliers du XVIIe siècle*. Paris: Nizet, 1972. Thoughtful situation of the quality of solitude at Les Rochers set against traditional patterns of meaning of withdrawal from the world.

VILCOSQUI, MARCEL. "Une Mélomane au XVIIe siècle: Madame de Sévigné (1626-1696), *Recherches sur la Musique française classique* (A. & J. Picard) 17 (1977): 31-93. Anthology of passages on music with commentary including sections on dance and "La musique utilisée comme procédé littéraire."

WOOLF, VIRGINIA. "Madame de Sévigné," *The Death of the Moth*. New York: Harcourt-Brace, 1942, pp. 51-57.

Index

DATE DUE
